Contents

Introduction

This second volume in Visions International's new series "The LT Area" looks at London Transport Central Area bus operations in South West London. By "South West London", I mean those parts of London south of the Thames with a SW postcode, as well as those parts of Greater London formerly in Surrey, for example Kingston-Upon-Thames and Sutton, with the Brighton Road as the dividing line between "South West" and "South East" London. For convenience sake, however, I have included in this volume the routes linking the New Addington Estate with the Croydon area as well as some districts, for example Epsom, which are beyond the former Greater London Council administrative area but were served by Central Area buses and, for that matter, are in many cases still served by London's red buses today.

Because of the meandering nature of the River Thames in the extreme South West of the former Central Area, it is somewhat difficult to draw a dividing line here, but generally speaking I have included such districts as Twickenham and used the Staines Road as the dividing line between "South West" and "West" London - Hounslow and Heathrow for example will be included in the "West London" volume.

As in the previous volume, most of the photographs from my archives included here I took between 1967 and 1984, though there are also a fair number taken in the later 1980s and the 1990s, plus a few taken in the present century to illustrate more recent workings. Most have never been published before, and they are arranged in various themes to illustrate the buses in their everyday environment.

An immediate difference from the previous volume (on South East London) is that there are fewer RT-types to be found here. This is because, by the time my photographs were taken, although still very numerous, they did not dominate the area to such an extent except in outer suburban areas such as Sutton. In addition, more Routemasters are evident, partly because they operated on trolleybus replacement services in the Kingston, Putney and Wandsworth areas and partly because a good few important trunk routes reaching the area received them quite early in replacement of RT-types. Moreover, also in the Kingston area, a considerable number of routes were operated by RFs rather than RTs owing to the preponderance of low railway bridges south and west of the town. Once again, although

Country Area services skirted the edge of the area covered, and reached into such centres as Croydon, Kingston and Sutton, I have not included these since they are already adequately covered in my recent volumes "Roadside with London's Country Buses and Green Line Coaches" and "Country Cousins".

As usual, my thanks must go to the P.S.V. Circle and the London Omnibus Traction Society from whose records much of the background information to the bus operations illustrated was originally gleaned, as well as to Ian's Bus Stop website for details of more recent bus types. Thanks go to Colin Clarke for scanning all of my 100,000 or so negatives ten years or so ago, Micheal J. McClelland for laying out the book and Ken Carr of Visions International for publishing this volume!

Jim Blake
29th February 2020

Although I've always lived in North London, when I worked for a few months as a conductor at Clapton Garage in 1974/75 one of my routes, the 22, took me into South West London. Here at its Putney Common terminus in the summer of 1974, I am learning the game with conductor instructor Morry Joseph (right). Driver Smith (left), whose forename I unfortunately forget, took us there and the photo was taken by my old friend Jim Owen. The bus is RM1554 (CT).

Main Cover Photo: Route 19 is one I've known since early childhood, serving my original home area of Canonbury and Highbury. However, it was also for many years an important trunk route crossing the West End and heading deep into South West London. On 10th April 1984, RM81 (B) is one of two on the route passing Clapham Junction Station and until June the previous year had been the Riverside Garage show bus. The 19 was cut back from Tooting Bec to Clapham Junction in 1987 (apart from Sundays), then to Battersea Bridge daily in 1991. However at least it retained Routemasters until April 2005!

Top Left Cover Photo: Kingston-Upon-Thames will always be associated with the RF class, which operated for more than 25 years on many routes in the area which passed beneath low railway bridges. Five weeks before the last was withdrawn, RF502 (K) departs from Kingston Bus Station for Staines on route 218 on 24th February 1979.

Top Right Cover Photo: Perhaps representing the lowest ebb of bus operation in the area covered by this book, a deceptively smart DMS711 (NB) loads up at Putney Bridge Station on 11th July 1987, a couple of weeks after L.R.T. cheapskate subsidiary Kingstonbus had taken over route 85 using DMSs resurrected from training duties like this one, or even reacquired from the Scottish Bus Group. The outfit was doomed to failure, precipitating the closure of Norbiton Garage just eight years after its £4m rebuild.

Back Cover Photo: It is often said that once Aldenham Works had been closed by the Thatcher regime's puppet L.R.T. quango in 1986, London 's buses soon visibly became very scruffy. However, there were also odd examples of this several years beforehand. One was RML2539 (NX) which heads out of Richmond town centre for home on route 37 on 16th April 1979. For some reason, it had missed an intermediate repaint in 1976/77, so not only was one of the very last Routemasters to retain a gold fleetname and numbers, but also has a balding roof and fading panels. Perhaps New Cross Garage's poor reputation for vehicle upkeep did not help, and the RML did not go to Aldenham for its second overhaul until 1980!

All-Over Adverts

Representing the all-over advertisement craze of the early 1970s, RM686 (SW) is in a light blue and cream livery promoting Vernon's football pools when heading north past Clapham Common Station on 29th July 1973. It had worked one of route 88's Sunday journeys to Banstead Hospital, where its bizarre livery apparently caused quite a commotion amongst the patients!

Also a Stockwell bus, RM783 (SW) advertises Uniflo anti-freeze in a basic grey and white livery, having traversed the delights of Brixton's Railton Road on 30th August 1973 on route 2. Today, of course, there are far more all-over advertisement buses on the road than there ever were in the 1970s.

One of the twenty-five RMs adorned in a special silver livery and renumbered as SRM1-25 to commemorate H.M. Queen Elizabeth II's Silver Jubilee in 1977, RM1871 (N), alias SRM7, tackles the one-way system around St. Matthew's Church in Brixton on 12th October 1977, shortly before being repainted red again. Each SRM had exclusive advertising, inside and out, for various companies.

Bank Holiday

For many years, special route 137A ran on Bank Holiday Mondays between Sloane Square and Battersea Pleasure Gardens. Buses were extras to route 137's allocation. On Easter Monday, 29th March 1970, RM458 (N) is about to turn around to return to Sloane Square after dropping off its passengers in Battersea Park. Of note is the LT Point Inspector behind it; he has been supervising operations.

Hampton Court Palace was, and still is, a popular tourist attraction and on Bank Holiday Mondays, extra buses were run on a number of routes serving it. One such was the 155, which was extended to Walton-on-Thames and then Hersham Station (latterly West Molesey) in replacement of the 131 on Sundays and Bank Holidays between 1962 and 1973. On Whit Monday, 25th May 1970, RT1926 (NB) is an extra running on the normally RM-operated Norbiton allocation, passing the main entrance to the Palace and surrounded by Bank Holiday traffic.

Trolleybus replacement route 267's Hampton Court Station terminus, on the other side of the bridge to the previous picture, is also busy with Bank Holiday traffic on August Bank Holiday Monday 30th August 1971, as RM1130 (FW) awaits departure for Hammersmith. The RF on the left, presumably on route 201, also attracts a large crowd of passengers.

The first official May Day Bank Holiday Monday, 1st May 1978, was a horrible, wet miserable day. Nevertheless, Bank Holiday extras ran, one of which was RM857 (X) which has terminated at Kew Green on route 15's Sunday and Bank Holiday extension. A friend and I were visiting such workings that day, but by now had given up the ghost and retired to a nearby pub! RM857 has subsequently (albeit in reality an entirely different vehicle thanks to the Aldenham overhaul system) been preserved and immaculately restored to original 1961 livery.

Route 15's Sunday and Bank Holiday extension usually continued to Richmond at this period, and on Easter Monday 16th April 1979, RM235 (X) loads up with a big crowd of people at the town's Wakefield Road bus stand. Subsequently, route 7 was introduced on Sundays and operated this extension instead of the 15.

Above: An oddity for several years was the extension on Sunday and Bank Holiday afternoons of route 28 from its usual terminus in Wandsworth town centre to Putney Heath. On Easter Monday, 20th April 1981, RM642 (WD) arrives at the latter's Green Man terminus. This was the last day these workings occurred, journeys on route 77A replacing them from the following Sunday. This RM is another to be preserved today.

Left: Once running daily through to Hounslow, route 73 was withdrawn beyond Richmond (and later Hammersmith) on weekdays at the end of 1966, but continued to serve Hounslow on Sundays and Bank Holidays until October 1978. It was then cut back on those days to terminate instead at Twickenham Station. On August Bank Holiday Monday, 30th August 1982, RM1100 (AR) has just terminated there on the last day they would do so. Also, this RM which had a Leyland engine and obsolete Sims electrical equipment was one of the first 200 or so routine RM withdrawals amid the infamous "Law Lords" service cuts on the following Saturday, and was scrapped not long afterwards.

Buses in Trouble

Above: Throughout their long lives, RTs were a thoroughly reliable class of bus, and the sight of one broken down was rare, right until the end. However, on Sunday 29th October 1972, RT4172 (AL) has broken down whilst working route 77C in Wandsworth Road, and has had to be rescued by one of London Transport's Thames Trader recovery lorries. It turns from Lansdowne Way into South Lambeth Road, after passing Stockwell Garage, on its way home to Merton Garage.

Left: It was equally rare to see a Routemaster broken down at the roadside, but on Easter Monday 23rd April 1973, RM1181 (NB) has not quite made it to Hampton Court on route 155, and in doing so made the Bank Holiday traffic queues trying to get there worse. Its conductor looks on as fitters try to fix the problem. In the distance, on the same route, a Bank Holiday extra RT follows.

Churches

On a clear, crisp 5th December 1970, RT1191 (TH) takes the sharp turn into Streatham High Road outside St. Leonard's Church on the circuitous route 115, which was "blessed" with O.M.O. SMSs four weeks later. Streatham was the mid-point of the route which ran from Wallington to Purley, with rush hour extensions to Whyteleafe at this period.

A contrast weather-wise is shown in this view of RT1377 (NB) heading along Carshalton Road, Sutton for Belmont Station on route 213, with the Church of the Blessed St. Mary at the Cross in the background, on very wet 20th July 1972. Route 213 converted to DMS O.M.O. a fortnight later, and following withdrawal this RT became a mobile classroom owned by the Inner Education Authority. It subsequently became a hen house on a farm near Waltham Abbey, was then rescued by members of the ill-fated Docklands Road Transport Museum and then exported to Guernsey where it worked as an open-topper. It subsequently went further afield to Malta.

Bank Holiday working RT344 (NB) lurches around the corner by St. Peter's Church, Norbiton as it approaches Kingston town centre on route 155 on Easter Monday, 23rd April 1973. The destination "Norbiton Church" was used for buses terminating at nearby Norbiton Garage.

The Church of St. Mary The Virgin stands at the south side of Putney Bridge, adjacent to the site of Putney Bridge bus garage, which closed in 1958. It forms the backdrop of this view of RML2585 (AF), about to cross the bridge on route 74 on 27th May 1974. RMLs had operated the route since late 1966, remaining until its conversion to O.P.O. in 1987.

On 5th March 1977, RF202 (AV) passes St. Stephen's Church in Cambridge Park, Twickenham on its way from Richmond to Hounslow. Introduced with RTs in 1970 to localise the Richmond end of route 203, the 202 converted to O.M.O. RF a year later. BLs replaced them six weeks after this picture was taken.

The impressive St. Mary's Church at Sunbury-on-Thames stands on the one-way system where Shillibeer-liveried RM2142 (AV) terminates on route 237 on 30th August 1979. Very unusually, this route which had for many years run between Hounslow and Chertsey using single-deckers had converted from RF to BL operation in April 1977, but only nine months later in January 1978 was withdrawn south of Sunbury, converted to RM operation and extended from Hounslow to Shepherd's Bush in replacement of route 117! This state of affairs remained until February 1987 when it converted to O.P.O. Latterly, route 235 has replaced its outer section.

On 20th August 1982, RM350 (Q) is dwarfed by St. Matthew's Church in the centre of the one-way system in downtown Brixton, where it has turned short on route 35 during its short-lived period of RM-operation re-extended to Clapton Pond. Having received RMs to replace RTs in September 1968, the 35 converted to O.P.O. in June 1986.

A fortnight before tram replacement route 109's conversion to O.P.O., RM2208 (TH) passes Streatham United Reform Church, which stood in the High Road between the bus garage and the ice rink, on 24th January 1987. All three establishments have been swept away in recent years by a massive redevelopment inspired by Tesco's, to prove that "money talks"! Meanwhile, RM2208 had borne Shillibeer livery in 1979, and was later preserved in that guise. It has recently reverted to standard red livery.

By April 1990 very few non-B20 DMSs remained at London's service, but one that was still struggling on was D1804 (AL) which had latterly been part of the ill-fated Kingstonbus set-up at Norbiton Garage. Following withdrawal in July, it passed to the Fire Research Establishment at Borehamwood, who made short shrift of it! This view finds it heading north up Balham High Road on tram replacement route 155, passing the Church and Convent of St. Anne Deprane.

Contrasts

In the evening rush hour of 20th April 1972, RT1816 (HT) heads towards Wandsworth Road through Vauxhall Cross bound for Clapham Junction on weekday route 168A. It provides an interesting contrast with the SMS on route 181 on the right, and the Maidstone & District dual-purpose vehicle heading for Victoria Coach Station on the left. The patch below the RT's offside side-light is where an "L" plate had been - it had been a trainer for some time before being returned to service in 1971. Route 168A was introduced basically replacing the 168's northern section in 1965, paralleling it on weekdays between Vaxhaull and Clapham Junction.

On route 44's last day of crew operation, Friday 16th June 1972, RT2629 (WD) has been curtailed at "Tooting Stn, Southern Region" (to quote its blind) and has set down its passengers in Mitcham Road, before turning right to stand alongside the railway. In complete contrast, DMS7 (S) is also terminating there on route 220, and appears to have had an interim repaint after almost eighteen months in service. Its adverts for the "News of the World" typify the "sensationalist" rubbish that rag was infamous for! Route 44 fell to the DMS next day. Seven years later, RT2629 was purchased by members of the North London Transport Society, for whom it operated trips to rallies and outings until 1985. It has only at the time of compilation of this book (November 2019) re-emerged from storage and will hopefully be fully restored to the rally scene!

On a bleak 10th February 1973, RML2733 (TC) departs from the Central Parade terminus on the equally bleak New Addington Estate, leaving XA21 (TC) on the stand. This vehicle, which with many of its fellows had inaugurated the limited-stop C-routes to and from the estate some three years previously, provides an interesting contrast with the RML, especially since the fifty XAs had originally been used on comparative trials with an equal number of new RMLs in 1965/66. The result, unsurprisingly, was that a further 450 RMLs were ordered and maybe even more would have followed (or perhaps more FRMs) had the government not forced London Transport to buy "off-the-peg" vehicle types. The disastrous MB, SM and DM-types were the result! Meanwhile, all fifty XAs were exported to Hong Kong a few weeks after this picture was taken, and mainly replaced by DMSs.

RM1102 (SW) is one of two curtailed at Stockwell Station on route 2A on 6th July 1973, where they arrive and are about to run in to the garage escorted by a FS-class Strachan-bodied Ford Thames minibus also running in from route P4 - a great contrast indeed! The latter route had been one of four introduced in various parts of London to assess the feasibility of running minibuses to "open up" previous unserved residential areas some eighteen months previously. They were an immediate success, and paved the way for many more such routes, most of which nowadays have normal size single-deckers. Route 2A, on the other hand, was withdrawn in January 1974 and its terminus at West Norwood, Rosendale served instead by journeys on routes 2 and, later, 2B.

RT3668 (A) heads north along leafy Aberconway Road, Morden on 23rd March 1973 running back from Epsom on route 164. Behind, in contrast, a new Leyland National "coach" follows on Green Line route 711, having recently replaced RFs. Although Leyland Nationals had successful careers with both London Transport and London Country, they lasted nowhere near as long, of course, as the RTs and RFs they often had replaced. Route 164 retained RTs until RMs replaced them in January 1977.

In some respects, the bodywork on MB and SM-types vaguely resembles that on RFs, perhaps because their blind boxes were of the same dimensions. However, that was where the resemblance ended! To illustrate this, RF443 (AV) on route 237 and SMS824 (FW) on route 285 stand together in the forecourt of Feltham Station, where they have both turned short on 26th August 1975. The SMS, one of the last delivered in January 1972, had a mere six and a half years in service. The RF lasted some 23 years, and these innings were typical of both types! The RF was later preserved, too.

The longevity of the RM family also contrasted sharply with the feeble performance record of the awful DMSs meant to replace them! On 1st June 1977, RM342 (TB) on route 119 escorts DMS543 (TC) working the 166, heading out of Croydon in Addiscombe Road. This DMS saw just seven years in service, going for scrap after its first certificate of fitness was up. On the other hand, the body on this RM had already seen more more than seventeen years' service, and would see several years' more, whilst the stocknumber survived into the present century!

On 21st August 1980, RM1693 (FW) passes Bentalls department store in Clarence Road, Kingston in the company of one of London Country's 1978 Plaxton-bodied A.E.C Reliance Green Line coach RS38. They provide an interesting contrast, the coach being part of London Country's effort to update and improve Green Line's image. It was to have a very short live, being withdrawn after catching fire in service in 1983 - but would only have remained in use a year or so longer anyway, since these vehicles were only leased to London Country for their first seven years' certificate of fitness. The RM was already (numerically) seventeen years old when this picture was taken.

This scene at Streatham Fire Station in Mitcham Lane on 22nd April 1982 shows two of the contrasting bus types that were delivered to London Transport in the latter half of the 1970s - E.C.W.-bodied Bristol LH BL46 (TC) working the 234A, and B20 DMS2288 (BN) on route 95. Route 234A had been much extended to replace the 115 a year previously, and its BLs were replaced by bigger LS-class Leyland Nationals two days after this picture was taken. The route however was withdrawn in February 1984. Meanwhile, route 95 had to suffer DMSs until Metrobuses replaced them in October of the same year. It had been one of the first two routes to receive them, in January 1971.

On August Bank Holiday Monday, 30th August 1982, Metrobus M226 (FW) working crew-operated on route 27 at its Teddington Station terminus contrasts with early-bodied RM248 (HT) on the same route. This was the last time route 27 served its traditional terminus here, latterly only served on Sundays and Bank Holidays, and also the last time Fulwell Metrobuses did so, as it was cut back daily to Richmond Station amid the "Law Lords' cuts" the following Saturday. The route converted daily to Metrobus O.P.O. in October 1986.

The main entrance to Clapham Junction Southern Region Station is being rebuilt as B20 DMS2496 (WD) loads up on St. John's Hill heading for Roehampton on route 170 on 3rd June 1983. A similar contraption illustrates this type of DMS' ugly rear-end design working recently introduced route 156, which had replaced the southern end of the 77A some six weeks previously, on the other side of the road. Both routes had to suffer these awful vehicles until 1991, whereas route 39 had received new Metrobuses to replace DMSs four weeks previously. One of these follows the 170 up St. John's Hill, providing an interesting contrast with the two DMSs.

Two Metrobuses, with M72 (NB) nearest the camera, contrast with RML2566 (AF) outside Putney Southern Region Station on 3rd June 1983. The second Metrobus, of a later batch, also has a different front grille arrangement to M72. The latter had been one of the first 100 to replace DMSs in the Kingston area in 1978/79, whereas that on route 264 is a new one which had replaced DMSs on that route earlier in 1983. The 264 had been introduced in April 1981, replacing the southern end of route 74. In further contrast, Metrobuses themselves were but a memory by the time route 14 converted from RML to O.P.O. in July 2005!

M45 (NB) is another early Metrobus, bearing their original livery with white upper-deck window surrounds which only the first few unfortunately carried before the remainder appeared in all-red, escorting a B20 DMS in the same livery and an all-red Metrobus over the railway bridge at Barnes Southern Region Station on 4th June 1983. It is working a "short" on route 72 to Roehampton, rather than going all the way to Tolworth.

B20 DMS2308 (WD) and RM2057 (WD) stand outside Wandsworth Garage on a drizzly 11th September 1983. The contrast in their body design needs no further comment, nor does the performance of the two vehicle types which in total numbered 2,646 and 2,760 respectively!

This busy scene at Clapham Junction on 10th April 1984 shows RM550 (B) running back to its garage on route 19 escorting new M977 (WD) which had entered service replacing DMSs on route 295 two months previously, as they reach the junction of St. John's Road and St. John's Hill. A third RM on the 19 brings up the rear. The two RMs will head straight across the junction into Falcon Road, whereas the Metrobus will turn left into St. John's Hill.

One of the last acts of the G.L.C.-controlled London Transport Executive was to order four different types of new bus to assess which was best to see off the remaining DMSs and, ultimately, to replace RM-types. These were Volvo-Ailsas, Dennis Dominators, Leyland Olympians and Mk2 Metrobuses. On 13th May 1985, M1442 (SW) - one of just two of the latter to be acquired - accompanies an RML at Roehampton, Danebury Avenue terminus. A further batch of this type of Metrobus was subsequently acquired for use on the Harrowbus network, but they were only on loan.

The type of bus chosen as London Transport's next standard vehicle was the Leyland Olympian, of which more than 300 were delivered to them and their successor London Regional Transport as the L class. On 3rd July 1987, RM1121 (AK) on route 49 is pursued through Tooting Bec Common by one of them on route 249, which had replaced the 49's eastern section in May 1971, originally using SMSs. Route 49 would convert to Metrobus operation just over a week after this picture was taken, and later gain Ls itself.

Viewed from the northbound platform of Putney Bridge District Line Station in November 1990, former London Country RML2347 (AF) bifurcates there on route 22's journey from Piccadilly Circus to Putney Common, and contrasts with a Suttonbus B20 DMS which has terminated there on route 93. Suttonbus was one of the "cheapskate" L.R.T. puppet operators, saddled with these contraptions in an effort to stave off route tendering competition - at the expense of their own staff who were paid less than those at "normal" L.R.T. garages. By now, however, these DMSs were on their last legs. In contrast, both the RML pictured and route 22 survived with them until April and July 2005 respectively.

Downtown Brixton is, as always, busy as RM6 (N) escorts one of the recent VC-class Northern Counties-bodied Volvo Citybuses working route 133 from Stockwell Garage past the Victoria Line Underground Station in June 1992. Route 2B was renumbered as 2 shortly afterwards, and then converted to O.P.O. in January 1994. RM6, numerically and bodily the oldest then in use, would go on to help bring the curtain down on regular Routemaster operation in London along this same stretch of road, on route 159 in December 2005.

The L class Leyland Olympians were some of the last non-low-floor buses to operate at London's service. Clearly showing the split-step entrance arrangement which these buses were the first to standardise in London, L191 (N) crosses the junction of Poynders Road and Atkins Road from Streatham Place on 11th June 2004 on route 417, which had replaced the eastern end of route 137 (initially numbered 137A) some five years previously. Behind it is a London United TA-class Alexander-bodied Dennis Trident working route 57 from their Tolworth Depot, representing the new generation of low-floor double-deckers.

Contrasting the old and new orders of bus operation in London on 22nd July 2005, RM9 (AF) is a guest working on the 22's final day of crew operation at the southern end of Putney Bridge, whilst the Plaxton "Pointer"-bodied Dennis Dart typifies both the new types of single-decker, and the many new routes they operate, working route 485 for Armchair Coaches. This former luxury coach operator was subsequently taken over by Metroline, whilst hundreds of Dennis Darts of this basic type have operated in London for thirty years, a few still surviving as this book is compiled at the end of 2019. RM9 survives as a special events vehicle for Go-Ahead's London Central and London General entities today too.

Curtailments & Short Workings

Perhaps as a result of being stuck in Bank Holiday Monday traffic on 25th May 1970, RM1093 (FW) sets off from Hampton Court through Bushey Park working short to Brentford, Half Acre on trolleybus replacement route 267, rather than going through to Hammersmith. The route converted to DMS O.M.O. in September 1971.

On another trolleybus replacement route, the 154, RT1282 (A) has unusually been curtailed from the west at Norwood Junction Station on 19th April 1973, some three weeks before this route too fell to the then apparently all-conquering DMS. Today, it ventures no further east than Croydon.

In the period covered by most of this book, late running buses on routes heading south to Richmond were often curtailed at Kew Green. This has happened to RM85 (V) which is set to run back to what was then still referred to on blinds as "Highgate, Archway Station" despite actually being in Upper Holloway, on a wet Easter Monday 23rd April 1973.

Belmont Road, Wallington is usually remembered as being the western terminus of Country Area route 403, as well as one of Central Area route 115's termini. However, sometimes buses on route 157 were curtailed there. This has happened to RT4212 (AL) on 27th April 1973, a fortnight before this route also converted to DMS O.M.O.

Unusually for a Sunday, RM1997 (GM) is terminating at Chelsea Bridge Road when passing Clapham Common Station on 29th July 1973. This is perhaps a result of a staff cut, which will mean the bus setting down its passengers there and then running dead back to Victoria, Gillingham Street Garage. Having received RMs in the autumn of 1964, route 137 retained Routemasters until July 2004 thus having them for almost forty years.

In tram replacement route 109's final spell of RT operation, RT3559 (TH) approaches West Croydon Station heading for Brixton, Lambeth Town Hall on 28th April 1976. This is perhaps a result of late running, and the bus will set its passengers down there and run around the block containing St. Matthew's Church and return south. Today, the 109 which once ran from Purley to the Embankment loop only runs between Croydon and Brixton!

A couple of weeks before route 264 converted from RF to BL operation, RF537 (FW) has been curtailed at Hampton Station on 3rd July 1976, and stands at a dedicated terminal stop usually used by buses on route 111. The 264 normally ran from Kingston to Hersham Station, with some regular journeys turning short at Sunbury. RF537 is now part of the LT Museum collection.

Route 71 (when running from Richmond to Leatherhead) had a number of scheduled short workings, particularly in rush hours. On 18th May 1977, RT734 (K) heads along Duke's Avenue, Ham bound for nearby Ham Estate, Beaufort Road working one of these. Behind, RT2663 (K) is running the full route through to Richmond. RTs were replaced by RMs on this route early in 1978, the latter remaining until ousted by Metrobuses in the summer of 1985.

On 25th March 1979, RM937 (AR) has unusually turned short at East Sheen, Black Horse on the 73's Sunday extension from Hammersmith to Twickenham. Of note are the two traditional red telephone boxes at this dedicated bus terminus, normal used by short workings on routes 33 and 37 at this time.

A road subsidence on Petersham Road, dubbed "The Petersham Hole" in the spring of 1979 led buses on routes 65, 71 and 265 to be terminated either side of it, and passengers having to walk between the two. With the Fox & Duck pub in the background, RM975 (K) is one of several RMs at its northern side, about to depart on a rush hour journey of the 65 to Ealing, Argyle Road. RMs had taken this route over from RTs in October 1975, retaining them until August 1985.

"The Petersham Hole" was still causing major disruption when BL53 (K) was setting off for the short distance to Richmond, Lower Mortlake Road from its northern side on 26th August 1979. The 265 had been introduced the previous 31st March, replacing the 71 between Chessington Zoo and Leatherhead.

Prior to route 137's exchange of routeings between Streatham Place and Streatham Hill Station with route 118, odd rush hour journeys on it terminated at Criffel Avenue in Streatham. On 4th February 1987 three days before the change, RML895 (CA) turns out of that residential street, which was a very odd place to have a dedicated bus stand for a major route, onto the main line of route in Sternhold Avenue, bound for Archway Station.

Down By The Riverside

On a cold, crisp Saturday 5th December 1970, RM358 (S) crosses Putney Bridge on trolleybus replacement route 220, to which numerically it had been new in July 1960. The route had been cut back from West Croydon to Mitcham at the end of 1966, and had several short-workings to Tooting Southern Region Station. It would be one of the first to receive DMSs four weeks after this picture was taken, along with route 95. These two routes met in Tooting - how wonderful for the passengers in that area to have the first new "Londoner" buses as they were initially dubbed...or maybe not!

Sunday-only route 19A followed the 19 from Finsbury Park to Clapham Junction, and then the 255 (which it replaced that day) to Hammersmith. It therefore crossed the Thames twice, at Battersea Bridge as RT457 (B) does on 28th February 1971, and then Putney Bridge. The route was introduced in February 1969 and withdrawn four weeks after this picture was taken.

On 27th April 1973, RM997 (NB) has just crossed Kingston Bridge when calling at Hampton Wick on route 131. This traditional route was extended from Kingston to Wimbledon in May 1962 to replace trolleybus route 604, and converted from RT to RM operation. A fortnight after this picture was taken, it received O.M.O. DMSs.

On the same day as the previous picture, RF421 (FW) crosses Kingston Bridge itself bound for Hersham Green on route 264. Of note are the trolleybus traction standards, still in use for street lighting long after the trolleybuses have gone. In common with most other RF-operated routes in the Kingston area, the 264 converted to BL operation in the latter half of 1976.

Traffic is brisk on Whit Monday 26th May 1975, as RM1083 (FW) works Fulwell's Sunday and Bank Holiday allocation of route 27 through to Teddington. Route 27 had been cut back from Teddington to Richmond on Mondays to Saturdays in June 1970 and also converted from RT to RM operation, with new SM-operated route 270 replacing its outer section. At the time this picture was taken, four different garages - Holloway (daily), Turnham Green (Mondays to Fridays and Sundays), Riverside (Saturdays) and Fulwell (Sundays) operated route 27! This was in fact quite typical of LT working practices at the time.

With the River Thames in the background and the beer garden of The Flower Pot pub beside it, RF432 (AV) heads through Sunbury Village on its way from Cherstey to Hounslow on a scorching hot 3rd July 1976. Two RF routes, the 216 and 237, met at this pleasant Thames-side village, the latter being subsequently operated by RMs as mentioned earlier.

Shortly after the appearance of a group of them at Victoria, Gillingham Street Garage to cover for RMs suffering from the vehicle spares shortage of the mid-1970s, RT4816 (GM) crosses Chelsea Bridge on 26th August 1976 nearly twelve years after route 137 had converted from RT and RTL to RM operation in the autumn of 1964. It would retain them until July 2004 - thus was Routemaster operated for almost forty years, as mentioned earlier!

On a very un-spring-like Sunday 16th April 1978, RM268 (D) runs alongside the Thames on Barnes Terrace, with Barnes Bridge and Southern Region Station in the background. The Sunday-only route 9A differed from the 9 in running between St. Paul's and Aldgate via Cannon Street and Monument Station, rather than to Liverpool Street Station via Bank. It was withdrawn in October 1978, when the 9 was rerouted daily to Aldgate, but reinstated briefly between January and April 1981. Today, it runs only between Aldwych and Hammersmith.

RM514 (R) has just crossed Hammersmith Bridge on 3rd September 1978, when working route 72's Sunday extension to Chessington Zoo. This route had converted from RT to RM operation in December 1975, and then gained O.P.O. LSs in January 1981. In later years, owing to the fragile condition of the ornate Victorian bridge, only single-deck buses were allowed over it and at the time of writing it is closed to all traffic except cyclists, thus meaning lengthy diversions to the bus routes that usually cross it.

RML2304 (AV) crosses Richmond Bridge on the busy inner-suburban peripheral route 37 on 3rd June 1982, just over four years before this route (at the time running from Peckham to Hounslow via Dulwich, Clapham, Wandsworth, Putney and Richmond) was ruined by being converted to O.P.O. and subsequently split into three overlapping routes. Of note are the dilapidated Georgian riverside houses on the left, which had been left empty for many years. Refurbishment of them is just beginning at the time, and they are now splendidly restored. Meanwhile, numerically RML2304 is splendidly restored too nowadays, in a blue livery promoting Millwall Football Club.

Autumn leaves fall around RM500 (HT) which has been curtailed at Kew Green on 24th October 1986, the last day of RM operation on route 27. Of note is the special bus stop behind it, which explains that it is alighting point only for buses terminating there. Numerically, RM500 was burnt out when working from the same garage in January 1968, but "saved" thanks to there being a spare "float" body at Aldenham, with which it emerged a few months later. Some twenty years after that, the RM bearing the number RM500 went for scrap!

On 26th June 1987, a somewhat unkempt RM255 (WD) changes crew at the southern end of Wandsworth Bridge, a couple of weeks before the nearby garage closed. However it was retained for use by the Sightseeing fleet, and remains in such occupancy today. Of note are the industrial riverside buildings behind the RM. Today, most of these have been swept away to make way for riverside apartments and so on, mostly beyond the reach of ordinary Londoners price-wise.

RM1971 (S) passes the pond in Barnes Green as it approaches the Thames on route 9's last day of operation to Mortlake, 17th July 1992. Part of the site of Mortlake Garage, which had closed in June 1983, was used as its terminus. The fragile condition of Hammersmith Bridge hastened the demise of this part of the 9's traditional routeing and next day it was cut back to Hammersmith.

Hills

Nicely illustrating the hilly nature of much of South West London, RT2468 (A) climbs up Ringstead Road, Carshalton on trolleybus replacement route 154 on 27th March 1971. It is only going as far as West Croydon, otherwise it would have an even steeper hill, Anerley Hill, to climb later!

Not far away, another long hill is Stonecot Hill, between Morden and North Cheam. On 6th October 1972, RT4234 (AL) is one of two on route 93 which appear to have this busy main road all to themselves. It is working Merton's Saturday allocation on this route, which was otherwise worked by Sutton Garage at this time. The route converted to RM operation daily in March 1976, having previously had them at weekends from Putney, Chelverton Road and Merton Garages at various times.

The mists are rising, the rain is falling and the wind blows cold across the bleak landscape of New Addington as XA24 (TC) sets off to climb Gravel Hill on express route C1 running back to its home garage on 29th December 1972.

Not far away from the previous picture, XA16 (TC) descends Gravel Hill on express route C2 bound for New Addington on 23rd February 1973, shortly before the entire XA class, including three which had passed to London Country, were withdrawn and exported to Hong Kong.

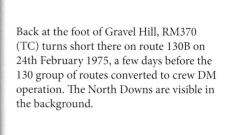

Back at the foot of Gravel Hill, RM370 (TC) turns short there on route 130B on 24th February 1975, a few days before the 130 group of routes converted to crew DM operation. The North Downs are visible in the background.

On 16th March 1975, RT2041 (BN) and RT2410 (BN) follow each other along Brixton Hill on the Sunday 57A, which now ran only between Brixton Garage and Thornton Heath High Street on the last Sunday of its RT operation - bunching on a Sunday? The route, which had once ventured as far out as Selsdon (replacing the 234 on a Sunday between there and Purley), converted to crew DM upon their takeover of the 133 the following Sunday.

RT2212 (A) crests Rose Hill in Sutton on 7th January 1977, just before routes 164 and 164A converted to RM operation. Both had been RM operated at weekends since the 93's conversion to RM in March 1976, but the 164 was converted to DMS O.P.O. and the 164A was withdrawn at the end of March 1979.

RM1748 (SW) climbs St. John's Hill, passing the site of Clapham Junction Station's booking office redevelopment on 23rd April 1981, the penultimate day of route 168's operation. It had only been converted from crew DM to RM operation in December 1980, and was replaced by alterations to route 77A, which paralleled it all the way from Westminster to Wandsworth anyway.

Five days before route 93 converted from RM to crew DM operation, a very full RM2002 (A) has reached the top of Wimbledon Hill on 30th August 1982, heading for Putney Bridge Station. As mentioned earlier, the route had only had RMs daily since March 1976.

On 21st April 1983, DMS1909 (ED) climbs steep Warham Road, South Croydon towards route 194's Croydon Airport terminus. Although this DMS was only some seven and a half years old, and had been overhauled in 1981, it was withdrawn three months after this picture was taken, although it lingered on as a trainer until early 1991. Route 194 struggled on with DMSs until the closure of Elmers End Garage in October 1986.

Somewhat confusingly, Brixton Garage is actually situated on Streatham Hill, and on 26th October 1984, RM686 (BN) changes crew outside it on route 133. Converted from RT to crew DM operation in March 1975, this route was only RM operated daily between 1981 and 1985.

On a very bleak 24th January 1987, RML2589 (BN) nears the top of Brixton Hill a fortnight before the 109 converted from RM to Metrobus and DMS O.P.O. from Brixton and Thornton Heath Garages respectively. RMLs were never scheduled for the route, this one being recently allocated to Brixton for the 137 at the time. Today, it is smartly preserved.

At the junction of Brixton Hill, Streatham Hill and Streatham Place, Northern Counties-bodied Volvo NV58 (Q) is nearing the southern terminus of the by now much-truncated route 45, at the junction of Atkins Road and Poynders Road on 22nd May 2004. Such split-step vehicles as this, delivered in the mid/late 1990s, had very short London lives indeed, due to the TfL diktat imposing low-floor buses on all and sundry.

A short distance from the location of both the previous pictures, RM2217 (BN) works the official last Routemaster-operated normal service of all in London at lunchtime on Saturday, 9th December 2005. RM2217 is numerically the last 64-seat RM built, and part of Arriva's heritage fleet. However, RM54 which was ahead of it and working through to Streatham Garage before working back to Brixton Garage ("Streatham Hill, Telford Avenue") from the south was delayed in doing so, and thus was the actual last one home.

Low Bridge Limitation

RFs were much more prevalent in South West London than in South East London owing to the number of low railway bridges in the area, which necessitated single-deck operation. An isolated example of this was route 234A, running from Hackbridge to Old Lodge Lane in Purley where on 31st July 1975, RF483 (TC) passes beneath the low bridge at Coulsdon & Reedham Southern Region Station. This route, as well as the 234 from which it was derived, also had a low bridge at Wallington Station until the bridge was dipped beneath it to allow double-deckers through in 1958. The 234A converted to BL in January 1977.

Most of the routes operated by RFs in the area radiated from Kingston, and were affected by low bridges on the former London & South Western main line, or its various branches. Route 201 was a typical example, and on 29th August 1975, RF424 (NB) passes beneath the low bridge at Thames Ditton Southern Region Station, on the Hampton Court Branch. The route converted to BL a year later, by which time Fulwell, Kingston and Norbiton Garages all had a hand in this minor local route on different days of the week. It no longer exists today.

Route 215 was similarly restricted by the low bridge carrying the London & South Western main line over Ewell Road, Long Ditton under which RF513 (NB) has just passed on 11th June 1976. This route too converted to BL operation, in October of the same year, and also no longer exists today.

On the same day as the previous picture, RF490 (FW) passes beneath yet another low bridge in the area of Surrey to the south-west of Kingston. This time it is on the London & South Western main line at Sandown Park, crossing Lower Green Road. Unlike the other routes in the area affected by low bridges, the 206 did not serve Kingston, but ran from Hampton Court Station via Esher to Claygate. In May 1962, it was transferred to the former Fulwell Trolleybus Depot when that converted to motor bus operation, since it was closer to the route than Kingston or Norbiton Garages. It was the first time RFs were allocated to a former trolleybus depot, and route 206 too converted to BL in August 1976 but no longer exists today.

Further out on the main line, the bridge at Hersham Station was a low one, too. On 14th July 1976, RF419 (FW) passes beneath it along Molesey Road five days before route 264, too, converted to BL operation. It too no longer exists.

The biggest obstacle to bus operation in this area was the bridge carrying the South Western main line over the old Portsmouth Road at Ditton Common (often incorrectly referred to as Littleworth Common, which is a little further south). This affected busy routes 218 and 219, running from Kingston to Staines and Weybridge respectively. They were deemed too busy to be converted to BL (which had the same seating capacity as RFs, 39) but the small Kingston Garage could not accommodate the longer LS-class Leyland Nationals. Therefore, in 1977/78, a number of RFs were refurbished and repainted to keep the routes going. On 30th September 1977, one of these, RF437 (K) emerges from the bridge heading into town. These were the only RFs to run in service bearing the then-current "solid roundel" livery, though some were also repainted carrying the old, underlined "London Transport" gold fleetname.

Having passed beneath the Ditton Common low bridge on 24th February 1979, RF511 (K) is working one of the many short journeys the 219 had to Hersham Green. By this time, the final solution to the problem of retaining RFs was solved by transferring the 218 and 219 to Norbiton Garage, where the larger LSs could be housed to replace them. This happened five weeks after this picture was taken. Routes 218 and 219 no longer exist as London bus routes in this area today, either.

Odd Men Out

One of the oddest cases of an unscheduled type of bus operating a route in South West London during the 1960s and 1970s was that of RTL418 (AF) being loaned from Cricklewood Garage to Putney, Chelverton Road Garage to operate Derby Day extras on route 93 on 29th May 1968. This view sees it heading back to Morden in Epsom Town Centre. Not only did it recall the days when all sorts of buses were summoned to work to and from Morden on Derby Day, but also the time when RTLs operated Putney's share of the route, before being replaced by RTs in 1965. Exactly six months after this picture was taken, the last of all London Transport RTLs were withdrawn from service.

Putney RTLs had also worked route 85, but were replaced by RMs in the summer of 1963. However, until the garage lost its small allocation of RTs on route 93 when it was cut back from Epsom to North Cheam in April 1970, these sometimes subbed for the RMs. RT2315 (AF) does so when heading out of Kingston a couple of weeks beforehand in the evening rush hour of 25th March 1970.

The busy 88 was another route which converted from RTL to RM operation, in July 1966, but RTs which had replaced RTLs on other routes at the garages which operated it, in this case Stockwell, could be found subbing for RMs until they themselves were replaced. Such is the case on 3rd April 1973 when RT3628 (SW) calls at Stockwell Station on its way to Mitcham.

Route 35 too had converted from RT to RM operation, in September 1968, and similarly, RTs still based at Camberwell Garage for route 172 subbed for them until their own demise nearly seven years later. One such instance is RT2631 (Q), passing East Brixton Southern Region Station on 1st February 1974 and turning short at Lambeth Town Hall, in other words St. Matthew's Church.

Just repainted and recertified for another three years' service, RT2240 (AL) heads along a remarkably deserted Battersea Bridge Road on 20th February 1975, subbing for an RM on route 49. This route had converted from RT to RM operation in May 1971. As for RT2240, it did in fact see another four years' service, ending as the penultimate RT in London Transport use. It was subsequently preserved, but ended up being butchered to form one of the silly "triple-deck" buses for a "Harry Potter" film in 2002.

Just along the road from the previous picture two days later on 22nd February 1975, RT2732 (WL) is another recent recertification and stands at route 45's short-turn (and at this time all-day Saturday) stand in Parkgate Road, Battersea. It too subs for an RM, this type having replaced RTLs and RTWs on route 45 at the end of 1965. Of note is the wartime prefab in this picture, still occupied nearly thirty years after the war had ended.

Typifying the RTs that were sent to non-RT garages during 1976/77 to alleviate the severe shortages of RMs caused by the nationwide shortage of spare parts at the time, RT4154 (TC) is a solitary example sent to South Croydon Garage for a few months in the spring and summer of 1976. It only appeared on route 190 and in this view passes an RT on route 109 apparently changing crew in London Road opposite Thornton Heath Garage. Quite what the SMS on the extreme right of the picture is doing at right angles to the traffic flow is anyone's guess!

The RTs sent to Gillingham Street to cover for missing RMs in the summer of 1976 stayed there through the winter and well into 1977. On 19th November that year, autumn leaves litter Clapham Common as RT1139 (GM) passes through on its long journey to what is still referred to as "Highgate, Archway Station".

Heading for the same destination on 5th March 1977, a very shabby RT2052 (HT) is one of a batch similarly sent to Holloway Garage in the autumn of 1976, which covered for RMs, RMLs and even crew DMs on most of their crew-operated routes for best part of a year. It has just set off from route 27's Richmond terminus and passes through the town centre.

Putney, Chelverton Road was yet another garage which received a batch of RTs for RM cover on route 30 in the autumn on 1976. They also subbed for RMLs on routes 14 and 74, and on 13th April 1977, RT4363 (AF) has very rarely worked one of the handful of rush hour projections of the latter route to Kingston Vale, where it stands prior to working back to Camden Town. The RTs were moved away from Putney Garage shortly afterwards.

For Derby Day, 1st June 1977, three RTs were loaned to Sutton Garage to work route 164A. One of these, RT2177 (A) which came from Bromley, heads away from Tattenham Corner on its way back to Sutton Garage. A fourth RT, RT1892 which had remained at Sutton when the 164 and 164A converted to RM operation the previous January, also worked the route that day as well as the 164.

Route 168A had been introduced with RTs in January 1965, linking Turnpike Lane and Clapham Junction Stations, replacing the northernmost parts of route 168 and the withdrawn 156. It was cut back to Finsbury Park Station from the north in September 1968 and then converted from RT to crew DM operation in January 1975, being subsequently rerouted to terminate at Hornsey Rise at its northern end. The unreliability of the DMs soon led to RMs and even RMLs subbing for them, and on 17th April 1978, RM102 (HT) has just set its last passengers down at Clapham Junction and heads up St. John's Hill to its stand. The route was never officially allocated Routemasters and was eventually withdrawn amid the Law Lords cuts of September 1982, curiously outliving the parent 168 by a year and four months.

In the latter months of route 77's crew operation, following the allocation of some weekday duties on it to Stockwell Garage in August 1985, RMLs allocated there for route 88 subbed for RMs. On 16th October 1985, RML2516 (SW) heads south along Wandsworth Road near to Stockwell Garage bound for Tooting. The route converted to DMS O.P.O. in January 1986.

Although RMLs had become allocated from Hackney Garage to route 35 at weekends following its conversion to RM operation in September 1968, a practice continued when the new Ash Grove Garage replaced Hackney in April 1981, they were not scheduled on weekdays. However, on its last day of crew operation, Friday 20th June 1986, RML2328 (AG) puts in an appearance. It passes Brixton Police Station, which is in the process of being fortified as protection against the frequent race riots in this area during the Thatcher years, and is nearing its Brixton Station terminus, which in fact necessitates the same turning and standing arrangements at St. Matthew's Church as the Lambeth Town Hall one illustrated on the same route earlier.

On 24th January 1987, RML2360 (CA) has just arrived at the temporary Streatham High Road, Green Lane terminus - which was actually adjacent to Norbury Southern Region Station - used between October 1984 and February 1987 while Streatham Garage was being rebuilt. Although showing an AK code, the RML is actually operating from Clapham Garage where it is based for route 137 and so is subbing for an RM. Route 159 was never fully RML operated though ended up with a mixed RM/RML allocation from Brixton Garage at the very end.

On The Common

South West London has a fair number of commons, giving much-needed green space to the area. On 9th December 1967, RT1535 (BN) calls at a snowy Streatham Common working what was then Brixton Garage's Saturday-only allocation on route 159, which was also extended on Saturdays from Thornton Heath Clock Tower to South Croydon Garage. No one could have foreseen when I took this photograph that exactly thirty-eight years later, Brixton Garage would work the very last Routemasters in normal London service on the same route!

Following its cut-back from West Croydon at the end of 1966, route 220 stood at Commonside West on the top north-west corner of Mitcham Common after terminating at Mitcham, Fair Green. RM323 (S) stands there on 25th September 1970, just over three months before its conversion to DMS O.M.O. Once again, this RM had, numerically, been new to the route in July 1960.

On 24th October 1971, some six weeks before route 64 also succumbed to the DMS, RM289 (TH) is at the junction of Carshalton Road and Croydon Road and about to cross Mitcham Common on route 64. This route had been extended from Croydon to Tooting to supplement the 220 when it replaced trolleybus route 630 in July 1960, introducing RMs (initially based at Elmers End Garage) to outer South London for the first time.

Clapham Common is perhaps the best-known of South West London's many commons, and on 29th April 1973, RML2393 (H) arrives there working Hackney Garage's weekend RML allocation on normally RM-operated route 35, with blinds already set for return north. The route converted to O.P.O. in June 1986.

RM182 (M) works a short journey of route 33 from Kensington, or perhaps only Hammersmith, to Richmond through Barnes Common on 18th October 1973. This route is of interest in that it had traditionally worked from Hounslow via Twickenham, Richmond and Mortlake to Hammersmith, Kensington and at one time even further into Central London, but was withdrawn amid the 1958 route cuts and replaced by an extension of route 73 from Richmond. However, at the end of 1966, the 73's extension was withdrawn on weekdays and replaced by a "new" route 33 following its original routeing. What made this especially odd was that another route 33, in the West Ham and Barking area, had only been withdrawn the day before!

For many years, route 93 has been the principal bus service through Wimbledon Common, and occasionally buses turn short at Wimbledon War Memorial, standing beside the common. RT2085 (A) does so on 5th June 1974, and it is to be presumed that the only "wombles" to be seen in the area at that time are those travelling on route 93 - between 9.30am and 4.00pm and between 7.00pm and midnight on Mondays to Fridays, and all day at weekends!

There is no snow on Streatham Common on a cold, crisp, sunny Sunday 9th February 1975, as RML2722 (TC) heads past on its long journey from West Hampstead to Old Coulsdon on longstanding Sunday-only route 59. Three weeks later, crew DMs replaced the RMLs from South Croydon Garage (derived from the 130 group of routes), though RMs from Streatham Garage co-worked the 59 with them. It was withdrawn at the end of October 1978, though the number 59 has since reappeared working daily along the Brighton Road, currently serving the Streatham Hill to Lambeth North Station section of the route

Spring is near as RM2203 (WL) heads through Clapham Common bound for route 45's Saturday terminus of Battersea, Parkgate Road shortly before this route also converted to crew DMs. RMs returned briefly between 1981 and 1985 before its O.P.O. conversion, and today route 45 is a shadow of its former rambling self, running only between Clapham Park and Elephant & Castle.

A couple of weeks before route 118 converted from RT to RM operation, RT3065 (BN) has just crossed the railway bridge at Commonside East, Mitcham on 22nd November 1975. The route converted to O.P.O. in the spring of 1985 and still exists today, albeit running from Morden to Brixton.

Route 155 was the last tram replacement route in South West London to retain RTs, converting to RM operation in January 1977. In their final summer of operation, RT2737 (AL) calls at Clapham Common Station heading for its off-peak and weekend terminus at Elephant & Castle on 16th August 1976. Of note is how the leaves on the trees are already brown as a result of that long, hot, dry summer.

On 24th March 1979, the last Saturday of red RF operation, RF481 (K) overtakes RF510 (K) at the northern end of Littleworth Common, between Esher and The Dittons, on their way into Kingston. Their replacement the following week would end nearly 27 years' successful operation of the red RFs.

On 23rd April 1981, RM830 is running back to Merton Garage on route 77's outer section between Tooting Broadway and Wallington, latterly operated separately from the inner part of the route between Tooting, Mitre and Central London. It has just crossed the railway bridge in Cranmer Road north of Mitcham Junction Station, at the western edge of Mitcham Common on the penultimate day of this working. On April 25th, new route 127 took over much of the 77's outer section.

As part of the "Law Lords" route cuts of September 1982, new route 60 replaced the northern section of route 130, between Croydon and Streatham. Initially, RMs were used but their tenure was short-lived: on 16th April 1983, RM2040 (TC) turns from Streatham Common into Greyhound Lane a week before the route converted to DMS operation.

The originally long route 65 passed through lots of pleasant scenery, much of it alongside the Thames between Kew and Kingston. Cut back from Leatherhead to Chessington in 1968 and then converted from RT to RM operation in 1975, it is still worked by the latter when RM995 (K) speeds through Petersham Common on 20th June 1983. By this time, the infamous hole disrupting the route just north of this point had long since been plugged. Route 65 still links Ealing and Kingston today.

Passing one of the ponds on Clapham Common, LS10 (AL) works what is left of route 189 on 10th April 1984. This had started life as a tram replacement route, running from Cannon Street Station in the City to Clapham Common replacing tram route 6 and then continuing to Raynes Park via Merton and Wimbledon to replace bus route 5, which had also paralleled much of the tram route. By now, it was just a local service which would be finally withdrawn after being reduced merely to school service in 1994.

Clapham Common still looks wintry on the same day as the previous picture, as RM1983 (CA) passes through on the 137's long trek from Crystal Palace to Archway Station. It is still looking smart after being repainted back into red after its stint in gold livery for LT's Golden Jubilee the previous year. Although the 137 retained Routemasters until July 2004, by then it ran only between Oxford Circus and Streatham Hill, having been pruned at both ends.

In contrast, it is a hot sunny day as RM359 (AK) passes through Tooting Bec Common on 3rd July 1987, a week before route 49's conversion to DMS O.P.O. This route also skirted Wandsworth Common on its way from Shepherd's Bush to Streatham, and today runs only between White City and Clapham Junction, the resurrected 249 covering the section illustrated here.

Route 65 also passed through Ham Common, as RM2035 (NB) does on 13th July 1985 having just called at the New Inn. Of note is the ornate LPTB wooden bus shelter on the right. The daily allocation on route 65 converted to crew Metrobus a few weeks later, though Hanwell Garage had a few RML duties on it on Sundays for a few months longer.

On 22nd May 2004, Arriva's RML2753 (BN) still looks quite smart as it passes the north side of Clapham Common on its way from Streatham to Oxford Circus some six weeks before the 137's conversion to O.P.O. Virtually all of the RMLs were refurbished between 1992 and 1994, but then had subsequent repaints and new "green" engines, right up to the time of their final withdrawal between February 2003 and December 2005.

Over And Under

Route 289 was introduced in June 1968, replacing the outer section of route 50, between Thornton Heath and Addiscombe. On 25th September 1970, RT1868 (TH) crosses the Southern Region main line to Brighton at the junction of St. James Road and Lower Addiscombe Road five weeks before the route's conversion to SMS O.M.O.

On 17th October 1970, RF457 (A) crests the railway bridge at Belmont Station on its way from Walton-On-The-Hill to Morden. Routes 80 and 80A had been converted from RT to RF O.M.O. in March 1969, and diverted north of Sutton to replace route 213A between there and Morden. Neither route had any low bridges enforcing single-deckers, their use was merely in the interests of economy and saving on staff. Today, route 80A has long since disappeared, whilst the 80 has undergone many changes. At one point extended from Morden to Putney to supplement the 93, the route now runs from Belmont to Morden, then continues to Hackbridge.

One of the few level crossings traversed by buses in the area this book covers is at Hampton Station, and on 27th March 1971, RT3797 (AV) negotiates it on route 211's Saturday extension to Kingston. This route was introduced in the summer of 1969 replacing the southern section of route 111 and running between Hounslow and Hampton Station using O.M.O. RFs on Mondays to Fridays, and RTs continuing to Kingston on Saturdays. It was withdrawn three weeks after this picture was taken.

Storm clouds gather above RT4430 (AV) as it crosses Richmond Bridge on 4th March 1972 working what was by now route 203's Saturday extension to Richmond, on the last day this was RT operated, since O.M.O. SMSs took over the following week. The route had been cut back to Hounslow on Mondays to Fridays in September 1970 and replaced on the section to Richmond by new route 202. Today, route 203 still links Hounslow and Staines via Stanwell.

On 10th March 1972, RT561 (BN) is just about the pass beneath the footbridge that had been erected across the High Road in Brixton when the Victoria Line station there opened in July 1971, having also just passed beneath the bridge carrying the Southern Region Kent Coast main line. Following the race riots here in the 1980s, the footbridge was removed since it provided an ideal platform for hooligans to bombard all and sundry passing beneath with missiles! Route 133 converted to crew DM in March 1975.

For many years, the railway bridge at Worcester Park Southern Region Station was too low to accommodate normal height double-deckers, thus obliging the 213 group of routes to be single-deck operated, although another route passing beneath it, the 127, did have lowbridge double-deckers (latterly RLHs) until its withdrawal in 1958. The road was dipped beneath it, however, allowing the 213 and 213A to be double-decked using RTs in 1963. On 20th May 1972, RT2251 (NB) passes through on its way from Sutton to Kingston. Both routes converted to DMS O.M.O. in early August that year.

On 6th June 1972, the bridge carrying the former London, Brighton & South Coast and London & South Western main lines over Falcon Road into Clapham Junction Southern Region Station nicely frames RT922 (B). It is unusually curtailed at Wandsowrth, Armoury Way on route 39, which also converted to DMS O.M.O. the following month.

RT2826 (AL) is nicely reflected in the waters of Carshalton Pond as it crosses the shallow bridge over it working route 77's Tooting Broadway to Wallington section on 16th June 1972. The 77 group of routes converted fully to RM operation eighteen months later.

Another case of a road having to be dipped beneath a low railway bridge was that of Manor Road at Wallington Station, which originally meant that routes 234 and 234A had to be single-deck operated. Its dipping allowed route 157 to pass beneath it using RTs, as RT3761 (AL) does on 23rd April 1973, some three weeks before that route too converted to DMS O.M.O. The 157 had previously been extended from Belmont Road, Wallington terminus (just north of the offending bridge) to Croydon and Crystal Palace to augment new route 154 when it replaced the 654 trolleybus in March 1959.

A week before the 77 group of routes' conversion to RM operation, RT4756 (SW) crosses the London & South Western main line on Durnsford Road bridge, Wimbledon on weekend route 77C. This RT was one of the 34 reacquired from London Country to cover shortages in September 1972.

"Now you see me, now you don't" was a nickname given to all-over advertisement RM906 (AK), which was adorned in a striking black and white-striped livery promoting Everton Mints. On 14th September 1974, it emerges from the shadows under the Southern Region Kent Coast main line bridge in downtown Brixton working what would become London's last normal Routemaster operated route some 31 years later.

Sporting a new coat of paint and still devoid of external adverts following a three-year recertification and repaint, RT2240 (AL) has just crossed the Southern Region Victoria to Brighton main line tracks at Tooting Bec Common, when subbing for an RM on route 49 on 20th February 1975. At this period, the failure of the MB, SM and DM families of buses meant that instead of replacing RTs, new DM-types were replacing MB and SM-types, meaning that the RTs had to be kept going, having initially been expected to all be withdrawn by about the end of 1974. In the event, they lasted until April 1979 and this one was the penultimate RT in service.

On 16th August 1976, RF440 (NB) has just crossed the bridge over the River Mole in East Molesey, a week before route 201 converted from RF to BL operation. Some such bridges in this area had weight restrictions, which also meant that heavier double-deck buses could not pass over them.

One of the furthest extremities reached by red "Central Area" London Transport buses in the south west during the 1960s and 1970s was Chertsey Station. On 16th April 1977, RF531 (AV) crosses Chertsey Bridge over the Thames on the last lap of route 237's journey there from Hounslow. The route converted to BL next day, but these lasted only until January 1978 when the 237 was extended from Hounslow to Shepherd's Bush in replacement of route 117, and converted to RM operation. As related earlier, however, it was withdrawn south of Sunbury and the section of route between there and Chertsey replaced by new London Country route 459.

Crossing the London & South Western main line bridge at Weybridge Station, recently refurbished RF516 (K) works the 219's rush hour extension to the nearby B.A.C. works on 6th September 1978. The repaint and refurbishment on this RF was done at Stonebridge Garage earlier in the year, featuring a then-current white roundel but traditional gold fleetnumber.

Some three weeks before Mortlake Garage closed, RM1438 (M) crosses Hammersmith Bridge on a drizzly 3rd June 1983. As related earlier, route 33 (by then running from Fulwell to Hammersmith and Kensington) had been withdrawn in 1958 and replaced by a westward extension of the 73, but was reintroduced at the end of 1966, with an eastward extension to Kensington on Mondays to Fridays. Converted to crew Metrobus operation and transferred entirely to Fulwell Garage when Mortake closed, it went O.P.O. in 1985 and still exists today running between the southern side of Hammersmith Bridge (due to the bridge's closure to traffic) and Fulwell.

Buses running in and out of Mortlake Garage on routes 33 (and the 73 on Sundays) had to cross the former London & South Western Railway Windsor and Reading lines by the level crossing at Mortlake Station. RM1325 (M) does so running out from the garage working short to East Sheen, Queens Road on 24th June 1983. This was the last day both of Mortlake Garage and of RM operation on route 33.

On 28th May 1990, RM1290 (GM) has just passed beneath the maze of tracks to the east of Clapham Junction Station in Falcon Road, when nearing route 19's southern terminus. Having previously continued to Tooting Bec, from which it was cut back on Mondays to Saturdays in November 1987, the route was further curtailed to Battersea Bridge daily a year after this picture was taken. However it retained Routemasters until April 2005.

Routes 14 and 22 retained Routemasters even longer, until finally converting to O.P.O. in July 2005. A week before this happened, RML2361 (AF) crosses Putney Bridge on 16th July that year. The 14 had been Routemaster operated since the autumn of 1963, initially with RMs and then gaining RMLs in the winter of 1966/67.

Pubs

Typifying traditional bus termini on pub forecourts, Saunders-bodied RT4656 (AK) stands on the cobbles outside The Greyhound opposite Streatham Common on 26th November 1967, working route 49's Sunday extension to Willesden Junction. Opened as a coaching inn on the Brighton Road in 1700, The Greyhound was rebuilt in the 1930s and is still going strong today.

At the Battersea end of Falcon Road, at its junction with York Road, The Princes Head was another traditional pub that was also a turning point for buses, as well as trams and the 612 trolleybus. Sadly it was demolished in the early 1970s to facilitate road widening, and although a new pub was built nearby with the same name, enforced closure after a breach of licensing laws in 2014 led to its demolition two years later, and flats now occupy the site. On 28th February 1971, RT4683 (B) passes the old building on its journey from Tooting Bec to Finsbury Park on route 19.

Wandsworth town centre was renowned for many years by being the home of Young's Ram Brewery, and consequently was also home to many of their pubs. On 20th May 1972, RM844 (WD) stands outside one of them, The Crane in Armoury Way beside the River Wandle, apparently while its driver "uses its facilities". It is a Sunday, and the bus has come from Putney Heath to where the 28 runs on Sunday afternoons, rather than the nearby Wandsworth Plain terminus it uses otherwise. The Crane is Wandsworth's oldest pub, dating from 1738, and is still thriving today after a recent refurbishment.

Dwarfed by tower blocks, The Meyrick Arms in Falcon Road adjacent to the Grant Road bus stand on the up side of Clapham Junction Station still exists today, presumably drawing its custom both from the local residents and travellers using the station. On 6th June 1972, RM925 (R) has just set off from there on the by now much truncated route 255, which once ran all the way from Clapham Junction to Acton High Street, via Wandsworth, Putney, Hammersmith, Brentford, Hanwell, Ealing Broadway and Acton Vale! It had replaced trolleybus route 655 in November 1960, and was withdrawn shortly after this picture was taken.

For many years, a bus terminus has existed on the north-eastern edge of Putney Heath, opposite The Green Man pub, a Young's house. Somewhat oddly, the pub sign is on the other side of the Wildcroft Road to the pub itself, part of whose beer garden is visible on the left. It is still going strong today, unlike route 168 on which RT4460 (SW) has terminated there on 22nd September 1972. This tram replacement route had been extended there from Wandsworth, and was withdrawn in April 1981.

The Dysart Arms in Petersham Road is one of many pubs situated along routes 65 and 71 scenic section between Richmond and Kingston. Also on 22nd September 1972, RT1706 (NB) calls there on its way from Chessington Zoo to Ealing Broadway. Of note are the red bus stop and green Green Line coach stop, both "requests", attached to the pub sign's post. Now called simply The Dysart, the pub still flourishes today.

Two or three weeks before route 157's conversion to DMS O.M.O., RT3365 (AL) has just passed The Cricketers pub in Wrythe Lane, Carshalton on 23rd April 1973. Sadly this traditional Charrington's house was closed and demolished in 1980 and housing now occupies the site.

On the same day as the previous picture, RT2776 (AL) passes The Junction Tavern at Raynes Park Station, having just set off from the nearby terminus on weekend route 77C on a short working to Whitehall, Horse Guards. Latterly renamed The Railhouse, the pub was closed in 2014 and awaits conversion to flats with shops beneath in the former bar area. Meanwhile, RT2776 had retained its original body, distinguishable by extra ventilation slats on its front dome, following a tour of North America when new in 1952, but lost this (to RT1708) upon last overhaul in 1968. Both were subsequently scrapped.

Somewhat oddly, new route 280 which replaced the Tooting end of routes 80 and 80A when introduced in March 1969 and usually terminated at Belmont Station still had rush hour journeys to Walton-On-The-Hill. On 23rd August 1973, RT4283 (A) works one of these and calls at The Cricketers pub shortly before its terminus, which was also served by Country Area route 416 on which an RF has just passed it. Its conductor dismounts to check their time in on a timing clock attached to the pub's outer wall. This traditional Young's pub, especially popular for its large beer garden, is still going strong today. Not so, of course, the RTs on route 280 - they were replaced by O.P.O. DMSs in January 1974.

For many years, buses terminated at The Mitre pub in Mitcham Road, Tooting, notably the main section of route 77. On 28th December 1973, RM1601 (AL) is one of two RMs which have done so. The route's terminus was altered to nearby Tooting Station in 1991, some five years after route 77's conversion to O.P.O. However the pub still flourishes, renamed for some reason as "The Long Room".

On a very hot 2nd August 1975, RF443 (AV) has just crossed Chertsey Bridge on route 237, and appears to be overheating. So was I by this time, so enjoyed a pint or two in the splendid Bridge Hotel across the road - it is still going strong today, too. At Chertsey, not only did the red RFs meet Country Area buses, but also those of N.B.C. subsidiary AlderValley, one of whose vehicles is behind the RF. This entity had been formed by a merger of former B.E.T. fleet Aldershot & District and Tilling Group fleet Thames Valley a couple of years before.

Another nice country pub on the outer fringes of South West London is the Kings Arms in East Molesey, where RF387 (FW) calls on its way from Hampton Court to Claygate on 29th August 1975. In those days a Courage house, this Kings Arms is still flourishing today, and is not to be confused with the West End pub of the same name and brewery in Poland Street where I enjoyed many happy hours in the 1980s and 1990s!

The Earl Spencer pub at Roehampton was well-known as a bus terminus for many years, notably for route 30 which came all the way from Hackney Wick and passed near my home in Canonbury. On 11th September 1975, RT2196 (R) passes it on its way from Tolworth to East Acton some three months before route 72 converted from RT to RM operation. Sadly, the pub closed in 2004 and has subsequently been used as a wine warehouse.

On 10th October 1975, a week before route 65's conversion from RT to RM operation, RT365 (NB) passes the Duke of Buckingham pub in Villiers Road, Kingston. This 1930s-built pub and restaurant still survives today, but as related earlier route 65 no longer ventures south of Kingston town centre.

The historic Ship Hotel in Weybridge town centre dates back to the 17th Century, and is still very much alive today. On 24th March 1979, a very well-loaded RF520 (K) passes it on its way to Kingston a week before routes 218 and 219 converted to LS operation. This was one of few RFs to receive a white fleet number when it was refubished.

The Spencer Arms on the northern edge of Putney Common was for many years (and still is) the terminus of route 22, at which all-over advertisement RM1237 (B) stands on 6th January 1980. For many years a Young's house, the pub is now a freehouse called merely "The Spencer" today. Route 22 no longer runs to distant Homerton, having been cut back beyond the West End in 1987, and recently rerouted from Green Park to follow the 25's old routeing as far as Oxford Circus.

The Kings Arms pub at Mitcham, Fair Green is a splendid late Victoria establishment and, part of the Young's chain, still going strong today. That is more than can be said for DMS384 (A) which, complete with a hole in offside of its front dome - a common fault with these flimsy contraptions - passes it on route 280 on 22nd April 1982, two days before the route was withdrawn between Belmont and Lower Kingswood. As for the DMS itself, despite only having been overhauled in October 1979, it was withdrawn in July 1982 never to run again, but route 280 had to suffer these contraptions until May 1991!

On 10th July 1982, RM66 (AV) runs around the block to terminate at Sunbury Village and return to its home garage. It passes the delightful Flower Pot pub, a splendid Thames-side former coaching inn still going strong today.

At various times in their final years of crew operation, after their cut-back from Leatherhead, buses on routes 65 and 71 had rush hour journeys, largely for the benefit of schoolchildren, extended beyond their usual terminus at Chessington Zoo to the Fox & Hounds pub on the Leatherhead Road. On a very wet 24th October 1984, RM1818 (NB) stands in its forecourt about to head back to Richmond. Route 71 converted to Metrobus O.P.O. in August 1985. Dating originally from the 19th century and rebuilt in the 1930s, the pub survives today renamed "The Shy Horse".

In Richmond itself, RM370 (HT) already has its blinds set for the return to Archway Station as it passes The Imperial pub in The Quadrant on 4th April 1986. Sadly, this well-known pub which dated from 1890 and had latterly been well-known for hosting such cabaret acts as Adrella, Dorothy Deprane and The Trollettes, closed not long after this picture was taken. It later became a Pizza express, then a Costa Coffee and finally an estate agents' establishment - how the mighty have fallen!

To end this section of the book, RM487 (S) passes The Sun Inn on Barnes Green on 11th April 1992, heading for route 9's Barnes terminus some three months before its cut-back to Hammersmith. The pub is doing a roaring trade, not least with myself and a couple of friends taking "pot-shots" at passing RMs and RMLs as we imbided, as it still does today. It dates back to the 18th Century and is now a listed building, marketed as a "gastropub". The RM was based at Shepherd's Bush Garage at the time covering for the refurbishment of RMLs.

Road Rail Interchange

Of the many interchanges between bus and railway services in the South West London area, that at Kingston-Upon-Thames is one of the most important. On a wet 29th December 1966, RM1888 (FW) loads up outside Kingston Southern Region Station on trolleybus replacement route 285, two days before this was cut back to New Malden from Wimbledon, Haydons Road Station. The route still links Kingston and Heathrow Airport today.

At Wimbledon itself, RT3545 (AL) passes the Southern Region station on 11th November 1967, on its way from Kingston to Streatham Hill, Telford Avenue (aka Brixton Garage). Being also the terminus of the southern branch of the District Line, this too is an important interchange, the more so nowadays with one of the branches of Croydon Tramlink also terminating there. Route 57 is actually slightly longer today, running from Kingston to Clapham Park, which is slightly north of its previous Brixton Garage terminus - the reason for this is lack of stand capacity at the garage.

When Morden Station was opened in 1926 as the southernmost terminus of what became the Northern Line, it quickly became an interchange hub with various local bus services terminating there and radiating from it, and others passing by. One of the latter was route 118, on which RT2084 (AK) passes the station, also on 11th November 1967. This route was cut back from Raynes Park to terminate at Morden Station in March 1969. It still runs from Morden to Brixton (instead of Clapham Common) today.

There are two important road and rail interchanges in central Croydon, one at East Croydon Station and the other at West Croydon. On 9th December 1967, shortly before replacement by new RMLs, RM1604 (TC) approaches West Croydon Station on route 130A. West Croydon Bus Station is just around the corner, and in recent years the addition of both Croydon Tramlink and London Overground services here has made this interchange much busier.

More straightforward is the interchange at South Wimbledon Station, penultimate station on the Northern Line's Morden extension, which in 1968 was served by such routes as the 57, 93, 152, 189 and 213A. On 15th July that year, Saunders-bodied RT1210 (A) passes on the 93. The 93 still serves the station today, running from Putney Bridge Station to North Cheam, but with journeys continuing to Sutton Garage rather than Epsom.

On the London & South Western's Windsor and Reading Lines, Twickenham Station is an important interchange with local bus routes, both those passing through - for example the trolleybus replacement route 267, and others that terminate there. On 1st July 1969, RT4467 (AV) has done so on route 110, and accompanies an RM which has turned short on route 281 on the nearby bus stand. The vehicle on the left is roofbox RTL68 which had been sold to White City Coaches the previous year. Route 110 still links Hounslow and Twickenham today, and has recently been extended from there to West Middlesex Hospital.

Further out, Hampton Southern Region Station provided interchange with various local bus routes. A packed RF450 (K) has just called there on its way from Kingston to Staines on the 216 on 27th July 1971, whilst an RT on the short-lived route 211 follows bound for Kingston, and will turn right onto the level crossing just out of the picture on the left. The 216 survives today serving the same route.

On 23rd July 1971, RT2755 (BN) passes Brixton Victoria Line Station, which has just opened. Just around the corner, local Southern Region trains provide interchange with both the local bus services and the new tube line. However, route 50 converted to DMS O.M.O. next day and was recast to run between Stockwell and Croydon, its Stockwell to Victoria section being deemed redundant by the new tube line. It was the second route to bring these monstrosities to Brixton! Having been chopped and changed since, the 50 again links Stockwell and Croydon today.

Tooting Bec Station is another on the Northern Line's Morden extension, which provides interchange with local bus routes, especially those crossing the alignment of the tube rather than paralleling it. Three days before one of these, route 19, converted daily from RT to RM operation, RT2837 (B) passes it approaching the route's southern terminus, with its blind already set for return to distant Finsbury Park on 9th August 1972.

On 19th April 1973, RTs still dominate the bus terminus outside Morden Station as RT3138 (A), one of the 34 reacquired from London Country in September 1972, sets off for Crystal Palace on route 154. However, this route, along with the 157, converted to DMS O.M.O. the following month. Another RT has turned short there on the 93, which converted to RM operation in March 1976. Meanwhile, the 118 which also terminated at Morden Station had done likewise in December 1975. This left just the 164 and 164A RT-operated there, and these too received RMs in January 1977.

A week before the 77 group of routes converted to RM operation, RT4368 (AL) calls at Earlsfield Station on 8th December 1973. This station serves local trains on the London & South Western main line, providing interchange with such bus routes as the 77 and 220.

Further out on the former L.S.W.R. main line, Walton-On-Thames Station also serves local trains. Hitherto not served by a major bus route, it had route 218 diverted to double-run in order to serve it in April 1976 and two months later, on 11th June, RF521 (K) has just called on its way from Staines to Kingston. This route became a Surrey Country council service ten years later, no longer therefore being part of the London Buses network.

A number of bus routes terminate at Hampton Court Station, at the end of the branch off the L.S.W.R. main line and on the other side of the Thames to Hampton Court Palace. On 16th August 1976, RF424 (NB) lays over prior to return to Kingston shortly before the route converted to BL operation. It too no longer exists as a London bus route in this area.

Sutton Southern Region Station is situated right in the town centre, and is served by many local bus routes. A well-filled RM1317 (A) calls there on 13th September 1978 on route 164A. This route was withdrawn at the end of March 1979, and the parent 164 converted to DMS O.P.O.

For many years, Kingston Southern Region Station was situated equidistantly between the town's two bus stations, one being directly adjacent to it, the other opposite and adjoining the bus garage. On 29th October 1982, DMS1936 (AL) has just left the former, working short to Tooting Broadway on route 57. Still looking smart a year or so after overhaul, the DMS was nevertheless demoted to training duties a year later, though subsequently resurrected 1987 for the ill-fated Kingstonbus outfit. It ended up being exported to Croatia and used as a mobile cafe!

Richmond Station is an important interchange between the London & South Western Windsor and Reading lines which pass through the station, and the District and North London Lines which terminate there. It is also served by most bus routes which pass through the town. On a sunny 23rd January 1983, RM874 (HT) calls there on the last leg of its long journey from Archway Station.

On the London & South Western main line, Raynes Park is also an important station, serving local trains on it, as well as those which branch off to Chessington, and various bus routes both to the north and the south of the railway. The latter side was the terminus of route M1, which had replaced the Morden to Raynes Park section of route 118 and the Morden to Hackbridge section of route 151 in March 1969, initially with MBSs. The route was converted to DMS in May 1974, and on 21st April 1983, DMS1845 (AL) sets off from its Raynes Park terminus. Two days later, both the route and the DMS were withdrawn. New route 156 replaced it between Raynes Park and Morden, whilst an extension of route 293 replaced the Hackbridge section.

Like Richmond, Putney Station, situated at the southern end of the town's high street, is on the London & South Western's Windsor and Reading lines and provides interchange with both local and trunk routes. On 12th June 1983, M67 (NB) loading up on a Roehampton "short" of the 85 is overtaken by D2591 (A) on route 93. The latter had converted to O.P.O. using these as part of the "Law Lords" cuts of September 1982, whereas the 85 lost its RMs to what was then O.M.O. back in January 1971, initially with SMSs.

Croydon's other main transport interchange, East Croydon Station on the former L.B.&S.C.R. main line to Brighton has changed much since I took this view of a battered DMS1960 (TC) loading up there on the main West Croydon to New Addington route 130 on 13th November 1983. Croydon Tramlink dominates the scene today, and has replaced the 130 group of routes and the Express C routes as the main mode of public transport between Croydon and the New Addington Estate, whilst the DMS perished long ago - being withdrawn shortly after this picture was taken. It did, however, see further use on LRT contract work with Metrobus of Orpington before finally being scrapped in 1993.

For several years, Clapham Common was the southern terminus of the City & South London Railway, before the branch was extended to Morden and eventually made part of the Northern Line. Providing interchange with the many bus (and previously tram) routes serving the busy town centre, the station is in a filthy state on 20th June 1986, besmirched with graffiti and fly-posting. This is the last day of crew operation on routes 35 and 37 which serve it: RM2080 (AV) overtakes another RM on the latter route, which is presumably a New Cross one route-branded for the 53. Fortunately, this historic tube station has since been cleansed of all that rubbish!

In similar architectural style of the other stations on what is now the Northern Line's Morden extension, Balham Station adjoins the existing ex-L.B.&S.C.R. one, providing interchange with Southern Electric local services as well as buses and, originally, trams. On 20th April 1990, RML2398 (SW) passes by on the now much-truncated route 88, running only between Clapham Common and Oxford Circus, with a Sunday extension to Marble Arch. Converted to O.P.O. in August 1992, the route somewhat bizarrely has since been extended from Oxford Circus to Camden Town and, lately, Parliament Hill Fields!

Although it has had an adjoining bus terminus for many years, Putney Bridge Station on the District Line is some distance from the bridge itself and the through bus routes which cross it. However, late in route 22's life as a crew-operated service, southbound journeys towards Putney Common were diverted to serve the station. On 16th October 1992, RML2422 (AF) is observed doing so from the northbound District Line platform. The green vehicle following is a London & Country Volvo Citybus terminating there on route 85.

On 20th August 2003, RML899 (AF) looks as good as new after a smart repaint - despite the fact that routes 14 and 22 will convert to O.P.O. less that two years later. Viewed from the window of the Railway Tavern, it has just called at Putney Station, now bearing the logo of privatised operator South West Trains.

Still looking quite smart just six weeks or so before route 137's conversion to O.P.O., RM1811 (BN) passes Clapham Common Station on 22nd May 2004. The distinctive original City & South London Railway dome on the tube station entrance is visible to the offside of the RM, whose nearside has been besmirched by graffiti vandals. Perhaps if their homes and possessions were soiled by such rubbish, they would think twice about inflicting it on others!

Roof Boxes

Right: A good sprinkling of roofbox RTs operated throughout South West London. One of these, Saunders-bodied RT276 (K), lays over in the Kingston Southern Region Station Bus Station on 29th December 1966, two days before this variant of route 65 was withdrawn. A new variant numbered 265 appeared at the end of March 1979, effectively replacing the stretch of route beyond Chessington to Leatherhead which the 65 and then the 71 had previously served.

Below: Also Saunders-bodied, RT3915 (AL) passes Morden Station on 11th November 1967. Of note are its upper-case via blinds, fitted when route 157 was extended to Crystal Palace in conjunction with trolleybus route 654's replacement, and the introduction of new bus route 154, in March 1959.

One of a handful of Saunders-bodied RTs given white fleet names (instead of the usual gold ones) upon their last overhaul cycle in the summer of 1966, RT1689 (AB) calls at Richmond Station on route 90's long journey from Staines to Kew Gardens Station on 25th November 1967. The 90 group of routes were operated from Twickenham Garage, which was closed in April 1970, with operations transferred to Fulwell (routes 90 and 90B) and Riverside Garages (route 290).

On 9th December 1967, RT4573 (Q), another Saunders, has terminated in the yard of Steatahm Garage, working Saturday-only route 159A. This differed from route 159 by following the Monday to Friday 59A's routeing through St. John's Wood rather than the 159's. With the parent 159, it converted to RM operation in June 1970, but was withdrawn at the end of the following October when the 159 itself was altered to take the same routeing as the 59A, which was also withdrawn north of Charing Cross.

On a very wet 3rd May 1968, RT1829 (TC), another of the few Saunders-bodied RTs overhauled in the summer of 1966 with white fleetnames, approaches West Croydon Station on route 166. This route, which ran from Thornton Heath High Street to Chisptead Valley, converted to SMS O.M.O. at the end of October 1970 and still exists today, continuing to Epsom.

In Epsom itself, Saunders-bodied RT4299 (CF) is one of a number of extras loaned for route 93 running back from the town centre to Morden Station after bringing spectators to the Derby on 29th May 1968. The 93was withdrawn between North Cheam and Epsom in April 1970, replaced by new MB O.M.O. route 293, which overlapped it from Morden.

On 10th June 1968, buses serving Wandsworth Road are for some reason diverted along South Lambeth Road and Lansdowne Way, where RT1900 (AL) passes London Transport's iconic Stockwell Garage heading for Tooting, Mitre on the 77. This view clearly shows the set-back offside route number stencil holder which immediately distinguished Saunders-bodied RTs from those with Park Royal or Weymann bodies.

On 15th March 1969, RT1205 (AB) changes crew in Richmond Road, Twickenham, just around the corner from the garage (which backed onto the Thames) in Cambridge Road. This was one of the first Saunders RTs to receive an overhaul in their final cycle, in March 1965, and therefore one of few to retain a cream waistband, since grey ones were adopted from April that year. RM1315 (M) brings up the rear on route 33.

Also changing crew, RT2447 (AL) stands beside the River Wandle opposite Merton Garage on 4th April 1969. This Saunders-bodied RT also had a cream waistband being one of the first to be overhauled of their final cycle. Route 152 was one of the last to convert from RT to conventional O.M.O. MB operation, in January 1970.

Running back to its home at Brixton Garage, Saunders-bodied RT2257 (BN) passes West Croydon Bus Station, also on 5th April 1969. This location has changed beyond recognition in the 51 or so years since I took this photograph, largely thanks to the introduction of Croydon Tramlink, but also because the bus station has been rebuilt twice. Route 133 has also long since disappeared from the area.

Route 85 had converted from RTL to RM operation in 1963, but the RTs which replaced Putney, Chelverton Road's RTLs two years later occasionally subbed for RMs on it. On 29th September 1969, Saunders-bodied RT3050 (AF), the only roofbox RT at the garage, does so when laying over between trips on route 85 at Putney Bridge Station. This was the last roofbox RT to run from the garage, which had had some of the very first ones, the 2RT2s, nearly thirty years previously.

Saunders-bodied RT1903 (AL) was the very last roofbox RT in London Transport service, probably because it had been fitted with saloon heaters upon its last overhaul, whilst all the others were not. On 25th March 1970, it heads along Malden Road, Cheam on route 151. This route had lost its Morden to Hackbridge section a year or so previously, and would be withdrawn completely three weeks later. Although a short section of it was experimentally reinstated, using RFs, in October in the Carshalton area, it was withdrawn for good in April 1971. RT1903 meanwhile perished a month before that, its withdrawal hastened by a rear end shunt which damaged its platform area.

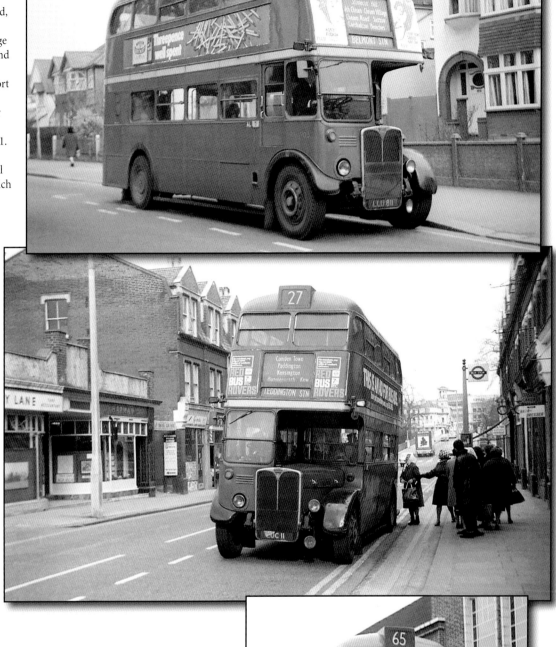

At the same time as route 151's withdrawal referred to above, route 27 was cut back from its traditional Teddington Station terminus to Richmond on Mondays to Fridays. With Richmond Bridge in the background, Saunders-bodied RT1931 (R) collects passengers on a Teddington-bound 27 in Richmond Road, Twickenham also on 25th March 1970. Route 27 converted to RM operation in June 1970.

On 28th March 1970, Saunders-bodied RT1252 (NB) loads up with passengers outside the Granada cinema in Clarence Street, Kingston on the busy 65. By now, withdrawal of these vehicles was well under way, and many more perished after the April 1970 route changes. Following those in June, just a handful remained in service.

Rush Hour

A number of routes in the area covered by this book had rush hour extensions. One was the 152, which was extended from Hampton Court Station to Feltham Station. On a murky 21st January 1970, RT2623 (AL) passes through Tolworth Broadway heading there three days before the route converted to MB O.M.O and this extension ceased. It was also rerouted from Tolworth to Esher, with route 72 being diverted to terminate at Hampton Court, with school journeys to Hampton Grammar School, instead.

Not actually a special rush hour journey this, but a busy rush hour scene at Putney Heath, Green Man as RM1386 (AF) collects passengers on route 85 bound for Kingston on 5th December 1970. The route gained O.M.O. SMSs at the beginning of January 1971, and still links Putney and Kingston today.

The New Addington Estate has an industrial area on its outskirts, to which rush hour journeys were extended on the 130 group of routes. In the evening rush hour of 27th February 1975, their penultimate day of Routemaster operation, RM358 (TC) stands at the Vulcan Works terminus ready for its return trip to Thornton Heath. The odd arrangement of two bus stops results from journeys to this terminus working from both directions.

In the evening rush hour of 11th June 1976, RF441 (K) calls at Walton-on-Thames Station where it collects homegoing commuters. The special board on the bus stop is explained by the fact that buses on route 218 double-ran to this station serving both directions, therefore it was necessary to have two separate stops, one for each.

By 18th May 1977, route 65 only continued from Ealing Broadway to Argyle Road in rush hours, and RT915 (NB) heads through Kingston town centre doing so. The 65 had converted from RT to RM operation in October 1975, but this RT was sent to Norbiton Garage in March 1976 as a spare, remaining there until September 1977 when it moved to Kingston for the 71 until that route too converted to RM operation in January 1978.

Trolleybus replacement route 281 had rush hour journeys extended beyond Tolworth Broadway to the Chessington Industrial Estate. On 6th September 1978, RM321 (FW) arrives at its Davis Road terminus there. This route would convert to Metrobus operation in August 1981. Latterly, local K-series routes from Kingston have served this estate.

Later the same day, RF516 (K), one of those refurbished to keep routes 218 and 219 going at Kingston Garage, crosses the London & South Western main line bridge at Weybridge Station, working one of route 219's rush hour journeys to B.A.C. Works. This establishment was better known for its World War Two exploits in aircraft production as Vickers Works.

Working one of route 74's few evening rush hour journeys to Kingston Vale, an almost empty RML2559 (AF) passes its usual terminus at Putney Heath, Green Man on 21st April 1981. Three days later, not only was this extension withdrawn, but the 74 exchanged routeings south of Putney Station and termini in Putney with the 30, therefore no longer serving this point, either, although terminating at Bessborough Road, Roehampton rather than the Earl Spencer.

DMS5 (AF) on short-lived local route 264 is the odd man out amongst three RMs on route 93 at their Putney Bridge Station terminus in the evening rush hour of 7th August 1982. RM463 (A) and RM1661 (A) are nearest the camera. Just under a month later amid the "Law Lords" cuts, the 93 will convert to crew D operation, and then to O.P.O. in April 1983. The 264 had been introduced in April 1981, replacing the southern section of route 30 between South Kensington and Roehampton, Earl Spencer. Also as a result of the "Law Lords" cuts, it was withdrawn north of Putney Bridge Station, disappearing altogether in February 1987 when routes 30 and 74 were both converted to O.P.O. and revised again.

Over the years, a number of express routes linked Croydon and the New Addington Estate. By 16th September 1982, a fortnight after the last of the "C" Express routes (originally introduced using XAs in 1970) had been withdrawn, DMS1862 (TC) heads into town on the newly-revived 130 Express service, which had replaced the C3, along Addiscombe Road. This service lasted until February 1987 when an X30 replaced it. Today, of course, Croydon Tramlink provides the fast route in this area. As for DMS1862, it was withdrawn in the autumn of 1983, spending more than a year in store before being used for training duties. It was then resurrected for the ill-fated Kingstonbus outfit for a couple of years, before going for scrap.

School Journeys

One of the most striking cases of a special working for the benefit of schoolchildren in the entire former London Transport Central Area in the 1970s was the extension of route 72 from Hampton Court Station to Hampton Grammar School, serving otherwise unserved roads at the latter. On 2nd October 1973, RT4120 (R) is working it when heading along Thornhill Road, Hook. Three weeks after this picture was taken, the route was withdrawn between Tolworth and Hampton Court, thereby bringing these journeys to an end too.

A similar extension was made to route 77A, from Raynes Park Station to Worcester Park Station, outside which RM71 (AL) awaits return on its long journey to Kings Cross on 4th May 1978. The extension, which ran via New Malden and routes 213/A, was withdrawn at the end of October 1978.

Route 33 also had special school journeys, which diverted from its main route in East Sheen via Clifford Avenue to travel to Richmond via Lower Richmond Road rather than Upper Richmond Road. Just under a year after they were introduced, RM1647 (M) heads along Lower Richmond Road on 18th September 1978. These journeys were discernable by special yellow destination blinds reading "Richmond via Clifford Avenue", as illustrated here. They survived the closure of Mortlake Garage and the 33's transfer to Fulwell and conversion to crew Metrobus operation in June 1983, but were withdrawn when it converted to O.P.O. in February 1985.

South West Suburbia

The area loosely described as "South West London" covered by this book includes Victorian inner suburban areas, outer suburbs that sprang up between the World Wars and also historic villages on its periphery. Battersea generally falls into the first category, but thanks to the ravages of the Luftwaffe in World War two, also contains many post-war flats. This view of RTL179 (B) heading south along Battersea Park Road bound for Southfields Station on route 39 illustrates this on 1st April 1967. Replacement of Battersea's RTLs by RTs was just starting at this time, and all were gone by early July, many resettled in the East at such garages as Bow and West Ham.

Passing a milkman's float, perhaps making deliveries to the nearby school before "Thatcher the milk snatcher" ended free school milk, RT1654 (AL) on route 200 heads along Queens Road, Wimbledon, one of a number of residential streets in the area served by bus routes. The date is 29th January 1971. Next day, passengers in this area suffered a double whammy - the 200 converted to SMS O.M.O. whilst the neighbouring route 189 had its RTs replaced by DMSs - the fourth route to get them.

The Roundshaw Estate near Wallington occupies much of the site of Croydon Aerodrome, and is reputed to be haunted by the ghosts of R.A.F. aircrew killed during the Battle of Britain. Be that as it may, the new estate was given new bus route 233 in May 1969, linking it with West Croydon and at first using just one O.M.O. RF. The following December, it converted to double-deck operation, using either an XA or the lone FRM. On 23rd March 1971, FRM1 (TC) heads along Mollison Drive out of the estate on its way to West Croydon. Four days later, the route converted to SMS. It later graduated to DMS and instead of terminating within the estate, continued to Wallington Station. It was withdrawn in April 1981 and replaced by a diversion of route 154.

Flanked by solid late Victorian (or perhaps Edwardian) housing, RT3473 (AK) escorts three others climbing up Broomwood Road towards Wandsworth Common on 13th May 1971, two days before route 49 converted to RM operation, and was also cut back from Crystal Palace to Streatham Garage. Today, this route runs only from White City (just north of the Shepherd's Bush Green terminus it had in 1971) to Clapham Junction!

Further out in South West London suburbia, RT1555 (A) heads along leafy Langley Grove in New Malden on 7th July 1971. Routes 213 and 213A had different routeings between New Malden and Kingston, this section of route being served by the 213A and not the 213, and both converted to DMS O.M.O. in August 1972.

Just under two months before their DMS conversion, on 16th June 1972 RM1238 (NB) heads for Sutton along Coombe Lane West, also in New Malden and served by the 213 and not the 213A. Norbiton RMs were scheduled to work the 213 on Sundays in the late 1960s, but by the time this picture was taken, it only ran on Mondays to Saturdays thus making this RM a sub for one of the usual RTs.

Close to the southernmost edge of Greater London, XA50 (TC) is apparently running dead off route 234 along Mitchley Avenue in the pleasant "commuter belt" suburb of Riddlesdown on 29th December 1972. Having worked this route for the previous three years, the XAs would be exported to Hong Kong in the spring of 1973. Route 234 was withdrawn in April 1985.

Not far away, most of the XAs operated on Express routes C1, C2, C3 and C4 linking central Croydon with the New Addington estate, which is virtually a new town albeit just within the Greater London boundary. On a drizzly 10th February 1973, XA6 (TC) passes the shopping parade in Arnhem Drive on the estate, working Saturday-only route C3. New DMSs began to replace the XAs a week later.

On an equally dreary 23rd February 1973, heads along Montacute Road nearing route C1's Homestead Way terminus in the New Addington Estate. By this time, the XAs were becoming very thin on the ground and all were withdrawn within a couple of weeks, being exported to Hong Kong in April.

Morden is typical of an outer suburban area built up between the two World Wars, its development stimulated by the arrival of the Underground in 1926. On 19th April 1973, RF438 (A) has just departed from the station and collects passengers on the other side of the road on route 80 bound for Lower Kingswood.

The suburb of West Molesey is well outside the boundary of Greater London proper, but is still served today by London Buses. For several years, route 131 which served it was replaced on Sundays by an extension of route 155 from Wimbledon, covering its whole route. On 23rd April 1973, some three weeks before its conversion to DMS O.M.O., RM997 (NB) and RM1219 (NB) arrive at the Central Parade terminus in West Moseley, both blinded ready for working short back to New Malden. Route 155 was withdrawn on Sundays upon the 131's DMS conversion, and (the opposite to the previous scenario) extended on Sundays to replace it as far as Clapham Common. Today, route 411 runs between West Molesey and Kingston, whilst the 131 has been pruned to operate between Kingston and Wimbledon only.

For many years, the residential area of Streatham Vale was served by bus routes 118 and 130. On 21st October 1973, RT4281 (BN) passes through it along Greyhound Terrace on the former route, which linked Clapham Common and Morden via Streatham and Mitcham. It converted to RM operation in December 1975, and then to O.P.O. in March 1985.

A little further south from the previous picture, a well-loaded RM326 (TC) passes a new housing development in Pollards Hill on 1st March 1975. This was the last day of full Routemaster on the 130 group of routes which, apart from a Sunday allocation on the 130 from Thornton Heath Garage which was still RT-operated until replaced by RMs in the autumn of 1976, converted to crew DM next day.

Surbiton is a well-known commuter town strategically placed on the London & South Western main line. On 4th May 1978, RM1091 (FW) has just called at the station when working trolleybus replacement route 281, bound for Kingston and Twickenham.

Walton-On-Thames is in the outer commuter belt, beyond the Greater London boundary and also situated on the London & South Western main line. On 6th September 1978, RF492 (K) does a U-turn outside it, when double-running off the 218's usual line of route in order to serve the station.

On 23rd April 1981, DMS277 (TH) passes Hackbridge Corner on the very circuitous route 115, which ran from Wallington to Purley via Hackbridge, Mitcham, Streatham, Thornton Heath and the Purley Way. It was withdrawn two days after this picture was taken, replaced partly by new route 127 and partly by revisions to the 200 and 234A. DMS277, meanwhile was withdrawn in June 1982 but did not go for scrap until more than eighteen months later.

Another DMS-operated route withdrawn in the early 1980s was the M1, which had been introduced with MBSs in March 1969 replacing parts of routes 118 and 151. On its penultimate day of operation, 21st April 1983, DMS1840 (AL) has just left its Hackbridge, Reynolds Close terminus and heads along Elm Road. This vehicle was withdrawn along with the M1, and used for a few years a promotional vehicle by the Greater London Council, seeing further non-PSV use with a number of owners well into the 1990s.

Route 72 converted from RM to DMS O.P.O. in January 1981, then two years later was jointly operated by DMSs from Shepherd's Bush Garage and LS-class Leyland Nationals from Norbiton - an unusual case of double- and single-deck buses being allocated to the same route. On 12th November 1983, LS294 (NB) departs from Tolworth Broadway bound for East Acton. By now, the DMSs had been replaced by Metrobuses and in February 1984, these took over the whole route.

Unsightly 1960s tower blocks in Roehampton's Alton Estate form a backdrop to this view of RML2586 (AF) at the Bessborough Road terminus of route 74 on 23rd July 1985, a fortnight before the route was withdrawn on weekdays south of West Brompton, ironically to where the RML is turning short from the south in this view.

Suffixed Routes

As elsewhere in London, a number of suffixed routes existed in South West London. One of the best known was the 77A, which ended up as the very last suffixed route on the London system, being renumbered 87 in 2006. Basically, the 77 and 77A ran together between Kings Cross or Euston to Clapham Junction, where they divided to go to Tooting and Raynes Park respectively, and were replaced at weekends by the 77B and 77C whose routeings between Westminster and Vauxhall differed. On Saturday, 18th March 1967, I am on my way from Nine Elms Engine Shed to Stockwell Bus Garage as one of the latter's inmates, RTL1234 (SW) heads north along Wandsworth Road on the 77C. It was withdrawn shortly afterwards and all Stockwell's RTLs were ousted by the end of August.

The 130 group of routes linking Croydon and New Addington had a complicated set of suffixed variations. One was the 130B, on which RM373 (TC) crosses Wellesley Road, Croydon into George Street on a very wet 29th September 1967 shortly before replacement by new RMLs. At the time, this route ran only on Mondays to Fridays, but it was introduced at weekends in October 1978.

A variation of route 65, numbered 65A, was introduced on Sundays in October 1963 replacing route 265, and running from Ealing to Chessington, Copt Gilders Estate. At the end of 1966, it was introduced daily (and the 265 withdrawn completely) and also extended to Leatherhead at weekends. For some reason, buses' front number blinds carried a large "A" suffix, rather than the usual smaller one, as amply illustrated by Saunders-bodied RT1701 (NB) crossing the junction of Petersham Road, Richmond Bridge and Hill Street on 13th April 1968. The route was effectively renumbered 65 at the end of November that year, but withdrawn south of Chessington Zoo.

A short-lived suffixed route serving the Brighton Road in the mid/late-1960s was the 133A. Originally running on Mondays to Fridays alongside the parent 133 from South Croydon Garage to Kennington, with a rush hour extension to Westminster, Horse Guards Avenue via Lambeth Bridge and Millbank, it was introduced in January 1964. At the beginning of 1967, it was shortened, and diverted north of Brixton, to Stockwell Garage. On 10th June 1968, RT3946 (BN) has just departed from that establishment, and is about to turn from Lansdowne Way into South Lambeth Road. The route was withdrawn five days later.

The 90 group of routes emanating from Twickenham Garage also had a series of complicated suffixed variations. As of 25th March 1970, when Saunders-bodied RT352 (AB) is crossing Richmond Bridge, the two basic variations were the 90 running from Kew Gardens Station to Staines and the 90B from Kew Gardens Station to Northolt, with a rush hour extension to South Harrow. The two routes divided at Hanworth, and by this time Sunday variations 90A and 90C had been withdrawn. Upon Twickenham Garage's closure three weeks after this picture was taken, both transferred to Fulwell Garage and received RMs on Sundays the following July, with the 90B converting to them daily in September 1971. They did not last long, however, as O.M.O. DMSs took over in January 1973. The 90B was renumbered 90 in 1989, the original 90 having been effectively renumbered 290 seven years previously.

Another suffixed route operated by Twickenham Garage was the 27A, on which RT723 (AB) has just run out from the garage into Richmond Road, also on 25th March 1970. The route had originally been introduced in October 1965, following the 27 from Teddington to Kew and then replacing the 265 between there and East Acton. In July 1969 it was withdrawn north of Richmond, then completely upon the closure of Twickenham Garage, effectively replaced by new SM O.M.O. route 270.

The circuitous route 115 had two suffixed variations, the 115A which replaced it on Sundays and the 115B which did so on Saturdays. On the latter, RT3845 (TH) awaits its crew in Thornton Road at the rear of Thornton Heath Garage on 1st August 1970. This route continued beyond Purley to replace the 234 along to Selsdon on Saturdays. Only introduced at the end of 1966, it was withdrawn at the end of October 1970. Of note is the large slipboard under the canopy of the RT advising intending passengers that the route travelled via Waddon and Purley Way, thus avoiding central Croydon.

Route 39A was a Saturday variation of the 39 which followed the parent route from Southfields Station to the north side of Battersea Bridge, and then replaced the 45 that day between there and South Kensington Station, rather than continuing to Victoria and the West End. On 10th June 1972, RT712 (B) heads along a remarkably traffic-free Falcon Road towards Clapham Junction, just over a month before the 39 and 39A converted to DMS O.M.O. The 39A had only been introduced in January 1971, received an extension to Putney Bridge Station in March 1973 and was withdrawn in October 1978.

Awaiting passengers and return north as far as Clapham Junction, RT3056 (AL) stands outside Worcester Park Southern Region Station on 6th May 1972, when working one of route 77As afternoon school journeys extended there.

A week before the end of route 90B's short-lived daily RM operation, RM1132 (FW) arrives at a very wintry Kew Gardens Station on 28th December 1972. Its sister route 90 had already been converted to O.M.O. in February of that year, but using SMSs rather than the DMSs which the 90B would be getting.

Gravel Hill, Addington, is equally wintry next day, 29th December 1972, as RM1744 (TC) heads for West Croydon on Monday to Friday route 130B. Although the 130 group of routes had officially converted to RML operation five years previously, such RMs as this frequently worked them until conversion to crew DM in March 1975. Not surprisingly, they were also often called upon to sub for ailing DMs after that, too!

Whereas route 85 had converted to SMS O.M.O. in January 1971, the associated 85A remained crew operated until March 1973. On 23rd February that year, RM179 (SW) calls at Putney Southern Region Station on its way from Roehampton to Putney Bridge Station, a couple of weeks before the route converted to DMS O.M.O.

On Sunday 29th April 1973, RM1780 (AL) heads along Garratt Lane passing Tooting Cemetery on the weekend 77B, on the last day this route ran. The following week, route 77 was diverted to run along Millbank and over Vauxhall Bridge, as the 77B had done, rather than over Lambeth Bridge and along Albert Embankment, thereby rendering the suffix superfluous. The route had gained RMs on Sundays following the 49's conversion to them in May 1971.

Starting at Morden Station, routes 164 and 164A ran through Sutton and Belmont to Banstead, where they divided - the 164 continuing to Epsom, and the 164A to Tattenham Corner. On Derby Day, 6th June 1973, RT1677 (A) sets off from the latter terminus amid the racegoing crowds for Morden. The two routes were jointly operated, which involved changing their blinds at the Morden terminus. Both converted to RM operation in January 1977, but at the end of March 1979, the 164 converted to DMS O.P.O. and the 164A was withdrawn.

Whereas the 77B was withdrawn in May 1973, fellow weekend variation 77C continued to operate until April 1981, differing from the weekday 77A by crossing Westminster Bridge rather than Lambeth. On 8th September 1973, RT4756 (SW), one of the 34 repurchased from London Country a year previously, crosses the tracks of the Southern Region West Croydon to Wimbledon branch at Merton Park Station three months before the 77 group converted to RM operation. When this route was withdrawn, a new O.P.O. Sunday-only route 77B replaced it between Clapham Junction and Raynes Park, only to be withdrawn itself two years later and replaced by new route 156.

Representing the Stockwell allocation on route 77C, RT2690 (SW) climbs a remarkably deserted St. John's Hill past Clapham Junction Station on 28th December 1973, a fortnight after the 77 group of routes converted daily to RM operation. RTs would, in fact, continue to appear on them until January 1977 when Merton Garage finally lost them from route 155.

Route 130B operated rush hour journeys to New Addington Industrial Estate. On 27th February 1975, RM410 (TC) stands at the Vulcan Works terminus there, three days before the 130 group of routes converted to crew DM operation.

Route119A was a Saturday-only variation of the 119, introduced at the end of October 1970. It ran between Thornton Heath High Street and Bromley North Station via Croydon, and differed from the parent 119 in running between Croydon and Thornton Heath along London Road, rather than the Purley Way. The route converted to RT to RM operation at the beginning of February 1975, as a result of route 47's conversion, but a month later on 1st March, RT2272 (TB) heads along Brigstock Road, Thornton Heath. RTs persisted on the route until the 119 itself gained RMs in May 1976. It was withdrawn in October 1978 when the 119 itself was rerouted along London Road in Croydon.

On 4th May 1978, RM2015 (SW) turns from Alexandra Road into Wimbledon Hill Road on the last leg of route 77A's long journey from Kings Cross to Raynes Park. In April 1981, the route was introduced daily between Kings Cross and Wandsworth, continuing to Raynes Park on Mondays to Saturdays. To complicate matters, school journeys and Sunday afternoon trips diverted off the main route to terminate at Putney Heath, Green Man yet retained the 77A number. Two years later, it was withdrawn south of Wandsworth except for rush hour journeys to Wimbledon, which in turn were withdrawn eighteen months after that. The route converted to D O.P.O. in April 1985, subsequently being withdrawn north of Aldwych and finally being renumbered 87 in June 2006.

New in June 1977 and one of the last standard DMSs delivered, DMS2243 (AF) calls at the Green Man, Putney Heath on its way from Putney Bridge Station to Roehampton, Danebury Avenue on 21st April 1981, four days before this route was withdrawn. The DMS itself lasted another couple of years with London Transport, and then saw use with several other operators, including Metrobus with whom it worked L.R.T. contract services, over the next twenty years. A rare achievement for this type indeed!

A peculiar development in April 1981 was the extension of route 234A, hitherto an insignificant local service running on the southern edge of the Central Area between Purley, Old Lodge Lane and Hackbridge, all the way from the latter point to Streatham Garage, replacing the western half of withdrawn route 115 and retaining the BLs which had replaced RFs in January 1977. On 22nd April 1982, BL58 (TC) calls at Mitcham Fair Green, two days before these were replaced by larger LS class Leyland Nationals. However the route was withdrawn in February 1984.

An oddity to grace route 77A in the mid-1980s was the unique dual entrance and dual staircase Alexander-bodied Volvo Ailsa V3 (SW). On 8th May 1985, it calls at Convent of the Blessed St. Maria of Ravensbrook in Wandsworth on its way to Euston.

Sunday Service

The 115A was a Sunday variant of the 115, introduced in November 1964 and differing from the main 115 by running via Carshalton Station on its circuitous journey from Wallington to Croydon Airport. On 26th November 1967, RM1360 (TH) is about halfway between its two termini when calling at Streatham Common. Along with the parent 115, it converted to SMS O.M.O. in January 1971 and was effectively renumbered 115 in October 1978, when the route reverted to its original self on Sundays in the Carshalton area, before its demise in April 1981.

Typifying how RMs not needed for their weekday routes on Sundays worked others usually the preserve of RT-types that day, RM729 (NB) arrives in Kingston town centre working route 213 on the same day as the previous picture. They officially worked this route on Sundays from December 1966 to March 1969, when it was withdrawn that day, but as illustrated earlier, occasionally subbed for RTs until the 213's DMS O.M.O. conversion in July 1972.

Also in Kingston that day, RM1238 (NB) has just called at Kingston Southern Region Station. At this time, Norbiton RMs working the 155 in replacement of the 131 on Sundays ran all the way from Hersham Station (also replacing the 264 at this extremity) to Clapham Common. When the 131 was withdrawn west of West Molesey in September 1971 (replaced by a new route 211 at its outer end), the 155 was cut back to there too on Sundays, finally ceasing to replace the 131 that day when it was converted to DMS O.M.O. in May 1973.

Sunday-only route 110A was a short-lived variation of routes 110 and 111 that day, linking Hounslow and Twickenham via Hanworth. Introduced at the beginning of January 1967, it was withdrawn in August 1969 upon the O.M.O. conversion and Sunday introduction of the 111. About halfway through its short existence, RM1098 (AV) arrives at its Twickenham Station terminus on 23rd June 1968.

For many years, trunk route 14 was extended on Sundays from Putney to Kingston, replacing route 85 that day and giving a through service all the way from Hornsey Rise. Latterly, a Norbiton allocation of RMs was added to the daily Holloway and Putney, Chelverton Road RMLs. On 5th April 1970, RM1536 (NB) speeds through Robin Hood Gate on the northern outskirts of Kingston working the extension. It was withdrawn upon the SMS O.M.O. conversion and daily introduction of the 85 in January 1971.

Another long trunk route from North London which had a Sunday extension further into the South Western suburbs was the 19, which received a Sunday extension from Tooting Bec Station to Streatham Garage, via Tooting Broadway to replace route 181 over that section, in January 1966. On 13th September 1970, RT1542 (J) takes the sharp turn by Streatham, St. Leonard's Church into the High Road. The extension was withdrawn in January 1972. Interestingly, the 19 had previously been extended to Streatham Common, but via the more direct route used by the 49, on Sundays for many years until 1957.

On the same day as the previous picture, and not very far from where it was taken, RT2410 (BN) heads towards St. Leonard's Church along Mitcham Lane on the Sunday route 95A. This differed from the parent tram replacement route 95 by continuing from Elephant & Castle to London Bridge (rather than going over Southwark Bridge and terminating at Cannon Street) and continuing to Aldgate for the Sunday markets there. Introduced in 1958, it had originally continued further, to Blackwall Tunnel, but was cut back to Aldgate in 1967. Originally RT operated, it received RTWs in 1963, being one of their last routes when converted to RM operation in the spring of 1966. In its last few months, RTs frequently appeared on the route as has happened here. It was withdrawn when the 95 had the dubious distinction of being one of the first two routes to receive DMSs at the beginning of January 1971.

As related earlier, route 90 received RMs on Sundays in July 1970, three months after it had been reallocated to Fulwell Garage upon the closure of Twickenham Garage. On 18th October 1970, RM1193 (FW) heads along Paradise Road, Richmond on its way from Kew Gardens Station to Staines. The route converted to SMS O.M.O. in February 1972.

A very peculiar Sunday-only extension, which took trolleybus replacement route 17 all the way through the inner South West London suburbs of Brixton, Stockwell, Clapham and Battersea to replace route 45 on Sundays, thus running throughout from North Finchley to South Kensington Station! The extension was introduced at the end of 1966, replacing the 45 throughout, apart from its Hampstead Heath section north of Kings Cross, which was covered by a new Sunday 63A. Four weeks before the extension was withdrawn and the 45 reintroduced on Sundays, RM627 (WL) passes Brixton Police Station in pouring rain on 20th December 1970, making this then run-down area look even more dismal and depressing than usual.

Originally a single-deck route linking Wimbledon Station and Raynes Park Station via Wimbledon Hill and the Ridgeway, the 200 received RTs in August 1965, and two months later received a Sunday afternoon extension to Kingston, largely for the benefit of visitors to Kingston Hospital. At the end of 1966, it received a weekday extension via Haydons Road Station and the new Fipps Bridge Estate to Mitcham, Fair Green. At the end of January 1971, it converted to SMS O.M.O. and lost its Sunday extension to Kingston. On the last day this worked, RT4465 (AL) loads up at Wimbledon Station, and incorrectly shows the "lazy" via blind for the 200's original short routeing. After various changes to termini, not to mention vehicle type, the route has settled down to run from Raynes Park to Mitcham since 1995.

A unique case of RFs operating a trolleybus replacement route took place in July 1969, when O.M.O. RFs from both Fulwell and Norbiton Garages replaced RMs on route 285 on Sundays. On 14th March 1971, the penultimate Sunday this happened prior to SMSs taking the route over daily, RF514 (FW) passes through Feltham apparently bound for Heathrow Airport North, rather than Central, its usual destination. Of course, the trolleybuses on route 605 which the 285 replaced never ran to that point, only going from Wimbledon to Teddington!

Of route 119's subsidiaries, the 119B was introduced at the end of October 1970 to replace the 194C in the Shirley area, thereby diverging from the parent 119. Almost a year after its introduction, RT3368 (TB) heads along Addiscombe Road into Croydon on 24th October 1971. The route converted to RM operation following the 47's receipt of them in late January 1975, converting to T O.P.O. in the autumn of 1984 but withdrawn a few months later as a result of route revisions in the area which led to the daily reintroduction of the 119.

A peculiar anomaly with the 130 group of routes, which had received RMs early in 1964 and then RMLs in late 1967, was the reversion of the 130 and 130A's Sunday Thornton Heath allocation from RM to RT, upon the garage's loss of RMs when route 64 converted to DMS O.M.O. in December 1971. On 23rd April 1973, a fortnight before this allocation ceased on the 130A, RT2284 (TH) heads along Gascoigne Road, New Addington, nearing the end of its journey from Thornton Heath. Bizarrely, a selfish motorist has parked his car, the only one in this immediate stretch of road, right on the bus stop which is itself obscured by the tree on the right. Route 130A converted to DMS O.M.O. on Sundays in January 1974, setting a trend suffered by many crew routes right up until the end of the last century.

Route 130 retained Thornton Heath RTs on the 130 for longer on Sundays, not getting RMs (from the long-protracted conversion of the 109) until October 1976, more than eighteen months after the main South Croydon allocation for the 130, which only worked on Mondays to Saturdays, had converted to crew DM! It was not until August 1978 that this type was allocated on Sundays from Thornton Heath, only for the garage to lose its allocation just two months later. On 21st October 1973, RT3559 (TH) heads along Addiscombe Road into Croydon.

As one-man, or as it became from 1974, one-person operation, spread, such types as MBs, SMs and DMSs allocated to routes that only operated on Mondays to Saturdays found themselves working normally crew-operated routes on Sundays, or in some cases shortened versions of them. This was in order to provide Sunday work for their drivers. An instance of this was the second version of a Sunday 19A, which replaced the parent 19 on Sundays between Tooting Bec and Clapham Junction, then paralleled it as far as Battersea Garage. Upon the 39's reintroduction on Sundays in October 1974, thus providing work for the DMSs and their drivers, the 19A was withdrawn and the 19 re-extended on Sundays. On its last day of operation, 29th September 1974, DMS407 (B) heads along Trinity Road, Tooting.

In contrast, route 57A was a traditional Sunday-only route, first introduced in 1955 running from Victoria to Streatham Garage via Stockwell. It was subsequently extended, first south to South Croydon Garage, and then also north on summer Sundays to serve London Zoo and Hampstead Heath, the latter point only being reached in 1959, with Camden Town being its northernmost terminus in the summers of 1960 and 1961. At the end of 1966, the route was withdrawn north of Stockwell but extended from South Croydon to Selsdon, in replacement of the 234, until August 1969 when it was cut back again. RMs appeared briefly in the late 1960s in place of RTs, but the latter returned at the beginning of 1971 when Brixton Garage lost them upon the 95's receipt of DMSs. In April that year, it was further cut back to terminate at Thornton Heath High Street, to where RT2813 (BN) is bound when heading along Green Lane on 16th March 1975. The route converted to crew DM the following week and was withdrawn amid the route rationalisations at the end of October 1978.

In similar vein to their working the 285 on Sundays, O.M.O. RFs took over the 71 from RTs that day in January 1971. On 27th July 1975, RF436 (K) heads along Star & Garter Hill, Richmond. BLs replaced the RFs in May 1977, but the 71's Sunday service was withdrawn at the end of March 1979.

In May 1975, route 72 received a Sunday and Bank Holiday extension from Tolworth to Chessington Zoo - a point it had also reached in the 1930s and during the war. On 16th April 1978, RM504 (R) heads for that point through Barnes Common. Surviving O.P.O. conversion early in 1981, the extension was withdrawn amid the "Law Lords" cuts of September 1982.

A somewhat odd Sunday extension to pass through inner South West London was that of route 49 from Shepherd's Bush to Willesden Junction, covering the 12 on that day and introduced in November 1958. On 17th September 1978, RM807 (AK) takes the sharp turn out of Streatham High Road by St. Leonard's Church at the beginning of its journey there. The extension was withdrawn six weeks later.

On the same day as the previous picture, RM69 (AK) heads south along London Road, Norbury on longstanding Sunday-only route 59. This had exchanged its southern terminus from Chipstead Valley to Old Coulsdon at the end of October 1970, and was also withdrawn amid the "Busplan '78" rationalisations six week after this picture was taken. The number 59 has subsequently reappeared daily along the Brighton Road, and today runs between Streatham Hill (Brixton Garage) and Euston, following the same route as the old Sunday 59 as far as Lambeth North Station.

Sunday route 9A was introduced in April 1971, serving the Tower of London and terminating at Aldgate at its eastern end, rather than Liverpool Street. On 22nd October 1978, RM1977 (D) passes the Sun Inn, Barnes Green on its last day of operation; the 9 itself being rerouted to Aldgate the following week. However, somewhat oddly, the Sunday 9A was reintroduced on 1st February 1981, but withdrawn again after Easter Monday, 20th April that year.

Sunday-only route 166A was introduced at the end of October 1970 using O.M.O. SMSs between Thornton Heath Garage and Chipstead Valley, replacing the 59 when it was rerouted to Old Coulsdon. It graduated to DMSs in January 1973, and on 4th May 1980, DMS1577 (TH) lays over outside Thornton Heath Garage. The route was withdrawn in February 1985, replaced by a "new" daily route 59, which was extended there on Sundays from Purley and ran via the 109's original route up to Blackfriars. Latterly extended to Farringdon Street, this version of the 59 was withdrawn in January 1994.

Illustrating the 131's Sunday extension to Clapham Common to replace the 155 that day, DMS2016 (AL) sets off from the Old Town terminus on 14th February 1982. These contraptions struggled on working from Merton on the route until June 1987, whilst the extension north of Wimbledon lasted until September 1990.

A short-lived Sunday-only route 77B was introduced in April 1981, replacing the 77C between Clapham Junction and Raynes Park and using O.M.O. DMSs. It was withdrawn two years later, replaced by new daily route 156. On 17th April 1983, its last day of operation, DMS2574 (AL) loads up at Wandsworth Plain. The RT behind is on an enthusiasts' tour.

On 13th November 1983, the Christmas decorations are up early on Allders department store in North End, Croydon as RM929 (TB) heads for Bromley North on the Sunday 119B. The route converted to crew Titans eleven months later, but was withdrawn in April 1985 upon the daily reintroduction of the 119. A new 194A covered the Sunday diversion via Shirley Way.

An oddity on route 88 was the appearance of a Sunday-only allocation from Merton Garage in April 1981, on which garage journeys ran in service beyond Mitcham. These became a regular service in February 1986, replacing route 200 through Phipps Bridge Estate. However, the route converted to O.P.O. on Sundays a year later. On 1st February 1987, the last day RMs and RMLs worked it, RM1708 (AL) calls at Clapham Common Station and illustrates the unusual destination display of Merton Garage (in small lettering) via Mitcham (in large).

Terminus

A well-known and longstanding bus terminus in South West London is Clapham Common, Old Town. On a dull and drizzly Friday 6th September 1968, RT2007 (T) awaits departure for distant Highams Park on route 35. This was the last day this old-established route ran north of Hackney, one of many drastically altered in the first stage of the ill-fated Reshaping Plan. The 35 was also converted to RM operation next day on "Black Saturday", 7th September.

Also on 7th September 1968, new route 290 was introduced to replace the various derivatives of route 90 between Hammersmith and Richmond, where RF488 (AB) arrives at its Wakefield Road terminus on 4th April 1969. It operative garage, Twickenham, closed just over a year later with the 290 and its small allocation of RFs transferring to Riverside. They were replaced by BLs in May 1976.

One of a number of traditional bus termini on the edge of the Central Area was outside the Midday Sun pub at Chipstead Valley. On 1st August 1970, RT1533 (TC) stands there on route 166, which was originally introduced in 1948 replacing route 59 on weekdays and running to Thornton Heath High Street. The route converted to SMS O.M.O. at the end of October 1970, and still exists today running from West Croydon to Chipstead Valley and on to Epsom and Banstead, providing new links which did not exist fifty years ago.

As mentioned earlier, traditional route 151 was withdrawn in April 1970, but owing to protests by residents in the Carshalton Beeches area which was left unserved, a shortened version of the route was restored between Sutton Garage and Belmont Station six months later, but only for a six month trial period. Unfortunately, it was not deemed worthwhile to continue it, so it was withdrawn again in April 1971. Three weeks before that, RF382 (A) leaves Belmont Station for Sutton - its driver has forgotten to change his blind!

A second terminus in Richmond existed at Dee Road, alongside the District and North London Lines just east of the station. It was used by buses terminating there from the south. On 2nd September 1971, RT2408 (AV) stands there on route 202, which had replaced the northern section of route 203 on Mondays to Fridays the previous October. The route converted to O.M.O. RF a year after its introduction.

Another bus terminus in the New Addington Estate was at Central Parade, from which XA21 (TC) sets off for West Croydon on 10th February 1973 on Saturday-only express route C4, shortly before the XAs were exported to Hong Kong and replaced by new DMSs.

For many years, route 157 ran in two overlapping sections on weekdays, Crystal Palace to Morden, and Carshalton, Wrythe Green to Raynes Park. On 11th May 1973, the route's last day of RT operation, RT3365 (AL) sets off from the Wrythe Green terminus for Raynes Park. O.M.O. DMSs took over next day.

One of London Transport's more bizarre bus termini was that within the grounds of Banstead Hospital, one of several former lunatic asylums on London's outskirts. For many years, route 88 was extended there for the benefit of visitors on Sunday afternoons, and on 29th July 1973, RM693 (S) is one of two on the stand. Otherwise the route was extended to Belmont Station, replacing routes 80 and 80A (later 280) on Sundays. When the 280 converted to DMS O.M.O. in January 1974, it was introduced that day, and the 88's extension withdrawn.

During the 1960s and 1970s, there were four different bus termini in the Clapham Junction area. One of them was in Abysinnia Road, a side street off Northcote Road just south of Battersea Rise. It was primarily used for buses on route 19 turning from the north, as all-over advertisement RM786 (B) has done on 2nd October 1973.

This scene on 8th February 1975 typifies the Clapham Common, Old Town terminus in the mid-1970s. Nearest the camera, RM1200 (AL) works the Saturday allocation on route 155, which did not receive them daily until January 1977 and RML2477 (H) is unusually working short on route 35 to Elephant & Castle from the south. This was also a Saturday working.

Blocks of former London County Council flats on Streatham High Road form a backdrop to this view of RT449 (BN) arriving at route 133's Streatham Garage terminus on 16th March 1975, a week before the route converted to crew DM operation. A yard at the side of the garage was used as a stand for buses terminating here, until the garage closed for rebuilding in the autumn of 1984.

For many years, route 22 has terminated at the Spencer Arms pub on the northern edge of Putney Common. A turning circle enables them to do so. On 16th April 1975, I have conducted RM1625 (CT) to it, and my driver the late Bert Barlow pauses our bus to enable me to record the occasion on film.

Thornton Heath Garage was rebuilt from a tram depot in 1951, and the forecourt of its main entrance in Whitehall Road is used as a stand for buses terminating there. On 1st June 1977, incumbent RM1448 (TH) on route 109 accompanies RT1538 (TB), which is subbing for an RM on route 119.

Belmont Road just north of Wallington Station has been used as a bus terminus for many years, with buses standing in the street. Before the road was dipped beneath the station bridge, all double-deck routes serving from the north terminated there. On 24th April 1978, RM1556 (AL) departs for a run back to Merton Garage on the 77's outer section, leaving SMS730 (TH) on the stand working the circuitous route 115. The following year, this SMS suffered the ignominy of being converted to the "Horse Bus Information Centre" parked outside Baker Street Station to promote the "Shillibeer 150" commemorative service.

Another traditional terminus is the dedicated piece of land behind Richmond Police Station in Wakefield Road. On Sunday 26th August 1979, RML2630 (HT) awaits departure for the long trip back to its home area at Archway Station on route 27, which had RMLs on Sundays from Holloway Garage at this period.

The site of the old Croydon Airport just off the Purley Way was the off-peak terminus at the other end of the 115. On 15th June 1980, SMS258 (TH) accompanies a DMS on route 194 there, some six weeks before it too converted to the type.

Epsom was, and still is, an extremity beyond the Great London boundary served by red buses. On 22nd April 1982, DMS1518 (AL) is at the terminus shared by routes 164 and 293 in the High Street. The 293 had replaced the 93 south of North Cheam in April 1970, paralleling it as far as Morden Station. Two days after this picture was taken, the route was reallocated from Merton to Sutton Garage. This DMS was withdrawn in September 1982, but saw further service with Western National.

Garages in South West London had the dubious pleasure of operating B20 DMSs for several years longer than any garages in other parts of London. One was Wandsworth, whose DMS2444 (WD) stands at route 44's Mitcham, Cricketers terminus on a wet 17th April 1983. The RT behind, RT2629, is on an enthusiasts' tour of routes it had worked in service, which included the 44.

On 21st April 1983, DMS2125 (TH) departs from route 64's Addington terminus at the foot of Gravel Hill, leaving two others on the stand. This route had the dubious "pleasure" of being DMS-operated from December 1971 to March 1992, for more than twenty years. A record for that unfortunate class, maybe?

In January 1983, route 216 which had for many years run between Staines and Kingston, was extended to Tolworth Broadway, following the former Country Area route 418's routeing. On 12th November that year, LS284 (NB) stands at the terminus just off the Kingston By-Pass. Leyland Nationals had replaced the BLs (which in turn had replaced RFs in September 1976) in September 1982. The projection to Tolworth was replaced by new route K2 in June 1987, and route 216 still links Staines and Kingston today.

Streatham Garage became the southern terminus of route 49 when it was cut back from Crystal Palace and converted to RM operation in May 1971. On 10th April 1984, RM740 (AL) arrives there after setting down its last passengers in the High Road.

Another of the terminal stands at Clapham Junction was just off St. John's Hill, to the west of the railway bridge crossing the Southern Region main lines adjacent to the Granada cinema. On 15th March 1986, RML892 (CA) has turned short there from the east. Although it shows the AK (Streatham) garage code, it is actually allocated to Clapham Garage, which reopened between 1981 and 1987 when Norwood and then Streatham Garages were being rebuilt.

Route 19's longstanding Tooting Bec Station terminus was in Netherfield Road, a residential side street. On 24th October 1987, RM2113 (HT) stands there prior to running back all the way to Holloway Garage. The route was cut back to Clapham Junction on weekdays four weeks later, with new route O.P.O. 219 replacing its southern section.

The 19 still ran on Sundays to Tooting Bec until May 1991, when the route was cut back daily to Battersea Bridge, which is still its southern terminus today. On 20th April 1993, three days before Kentishbus took over the route, RM843 (GM) stands at its terminus there - waste ground at the back of Battersea Garage which had closed in 1985 for service buses, then been used for another two years or so for the Sightseeing fleet. The building behind the RM is the former garage, closed by the L.R.T. regime only a few years after being substantially rebuilt.

By 20th July 2003, RMs and RMLs operating the 19 were housed in a ramshackle shed in Hester Road, Battersea, where they also terminated. It was opposite the site of the main part of the former L.T. garage, now demolished. Luxury riverside "apartments" are being built in this view to yuppify the area. RML2531 (BA) sets off for Finsbury Park and has been rebuilt with non-opening front windows following an accident.

In their last few years of crew operation, three of the four trunk routes linking Putney with Central London terminated at Putney Heath, Green Man at different times - the 14, 30 and 74. The 14 was the last to do so, and on 16th April 2005, RML2345 (AF) sets off from there for Tottenham Court Road, just over three months before the 14's O.P.O. conversion. This RML had gained fame in the late 1970s by being cannibalised to become an engineless hulk at London Country's Grays Garage, but was rescued by L.T. and reassembled at Aldenham Works, becoming the last ex-Country RML to be overhauled in red.

Town Centre

Just over two months after route 33's reintroduction, RM1543 (M) waits at the traffic lights in Twickenham town centre to turn right on its way from Hammersmith to Hounslow on 4th March 1967. A Twickehnam RT follows on the 90 bound for Staines.

Saunders-bodied RT1394 (A) completes a typical 1960's scene as it heads along Sutton High Street on route 80A on 11th November 1967. This route ran from Tooting Broadway to Walton-On-The-Hill, beyond the Greater London boundary. It was altered in March 1969 to run from Sutton via the former 213A routeing to Morden and converted to RF O.M.O.

On 15th July 1968, RF490 (TC) heads south along the Brighton Road through Purley Cross on local route 234A, which ran between Hackbridge and Old Lodge Lane. Although it is one-man-operated, the RF does not have the usual "Pay as you enter" sign on the front, and also has its platform doors open, perhaps because it is a hot day.

RT3797 (AV) has just set off from Kingston Bus Station for its home town of Hounslow, on the Saturday extension of short-lived route 211. It heads along Clarence Street on the one way system in the town centre on 19th September 1970.

With the famous clocktower in the background, RT392 (TH) has just set down its last passengers in Thornton Heath High Street before running to the stand in Zion Place on 2nd May 1971. The 133 was withdrawn south of Streatham Garage the following July.

On 14th July 1972, the day before route 39 converted to DMS O.M.O., RT4442 (B) heads along Wandsworth High Street bound for Southfields. At the time, the town centre here was dominated by Young's Brewery, as illustrated by the sign above the Midland Bank on the right.

On 9th August 1972, RT3761 (AL) heads south along Tooting High Road and is just about to pass Tooting Bec Station. At this time, route 155 literally ran above the Northern Line all the way from Elephant & Castle to South Wimbledon Station! It still runs from the Elephant to Tooting today.

An oddity in South West London for several years was the operation of the short 235 route between Richmond Station and Richmond Hill by private operator Continental Pioneer, who took it over when London Transport withdrew it in 1966. Typical of ex-LT and London Country vehicles used on it is ex-Country RF575, heading along Paradise Road in Richmond on 22nd September 1972. The working was withdrawn when route 71 was rerouted to serve Richmond Hill in 1980.

Several bus routes meet at Fair Green, in the centre of Mitcham. On 28th December 1973, RT2338 (A) on route 280 overtakes RT2542 (SW) on the 88. The latter is subbing for an RM, whilst route 280 will convert to DMS O.M.O. a week later.

With Allders department store behind them, RT1191 (TH) on route 109 escorts two RMs past the historic almshouses in North End, Croydon on 17th April 1976. RT-types had worked the busy 109 for over 25 years since it replaced tram routes 16 and 18, but a long-drawn-out phased conversion to RM operation was now about to begin.

Another famous department store was Arding & Hobbs at Clapham Junction, outside which RML2746 (SW) calls on route 37 on 20th October 1977. It is working short to Brixton town centre rather than going through to Peckham.

At Tooting Broadway on 3rd September 1978, RM702 (AL) overtakes DMS2285 (S) on route 220, having just set off from Tooting, Mitre terminus for its journey to Euston. Also of note is the yellow Post Office Telecommunications van on the left, soon to be rebranded British Telecom and then privatised by the Thatcher regime.

On 22nd April 1982, DMS1915 (AK) has just turned into Streatham High Road and is about to pass Streatham Station on route 249, which had replaced the eastern section of the 49 to Crystal Palace in May 1971, also paralleling it from Battersea to Streatham. The route had been withdrawn north of Clapham Junction in 1978, and then was taken off completely in 1989, replaced by a re-extension of the 49. However, a new route 249 has since been reintroduced in the Crystal Palace area. On this occasion, the bus has been curtailed to Crown Point in Norwood.

Late in their careers, when those originally designated "DM" for crew operation became O.P.O. vehicles too, many former DMs and DMSs were reclassified simply "D". However, oddly, some were also branded "DS". One example was DS2286 (BN) which heads along Stockwell Road into Brixton town centre on 30th July 1983 on route 50, which had converted from RT to DMS O.M.O. twelve years before. It wrongly shows a via blind for route 95, but does correctly have the "pay driver" flap on the front, this was reversible to show "Pay conductor" when the bus was crew-operated, as it could be on routes 109 and 133 at the time.

On 10th April 1984, L1 (SW) contrasts with an RM as it heads down St. John's Hill past Clapham Junction Station on route 170. This was one of three Leyland Olympians trialled alongside Volvo Ailsas, Mark 2 Metrobuses and Dennis Dominators as possible replacements for the remaining DMSs, and ultimately perhaps RM-types. Olympians were chosen as the next standard London Transport vehicle, though the vast majority were delivered after the Thatcher regime had destroyed L.T. More than 300 saw London service eventually.

On 11th November 1984, RM105 (BN) passes St. Leonard's Church in Streatham High Road on route 118's somewhat circuitous route from Clapham Common to Morden Station. The route had converted from RT to RM operation in December 1975, then went O.P.O. in March 1985. The route has subsequently lost its Streatham Hill to Clapham Common section, and today terminates at Brixton Station instead.

On route 109's stand outside the Post Office in Purley town centre just off the main Brighton Road, RM106 (TH) awaits departure for Trafalgar Square on 26th January 1985, during the route's second spell of RM operation, which had been from the summer of 1981 at Brixton, but not until September 1982 from Thornton Heath. Crew DMs had worked in the meantime from 1978, meaning that RMs had only operated initially for a couple of years when they replaced RTs two years previously. The 109 converted to O.P.O. just over two years after this picture was taken, and today runs only from Croydon to Brixton.

With driver Keith Molloy at the wheel on route 37's last day of RM operation, 20th June 1986, RM2013 (NX) passes Clapham Common Station working short to Putney. This inner-suburban peripheral route, whose full length was all the way from Peckham to Hounslow, was ruined next day by being converted to O.P.O. and later split into three overlapping routes.

On the same day as the previous picture, Brixton town centre is unusually quiet as RM109 (Q) heads south for Crystal Palace on route 3. Of note are the route change posters stuck inside the nearside canopy window, one of which forewarns of the 35's conversion to O.P.O., which also took place next day. The 3 itself would retain RMs until the end of 1992 when it to fell to O.P.O.

In the spring of 1994, shortly prior to privatisation, L.R.T. subsidiary South London Buses won route 159 on tender. Operation was transferred entirely to Brixton Garage with RMs, which were adorned in a customised red and cream livery, not dissimilar to that once carried by Brighton, Hove & District buses. On 18th March 1994, RM1593 (BN) approaches Streatham Hill Station. However, the buses were painted standard red again just three years later. No one then could have guessed that this would be the last fully Routemaster operated service more than fifteen years after this picture was taken!

Typifying the first generation of low-floor double-deckers, London General Wright "Gemini Eclipse"-bodied Volvo WVL15 (AF) sets off on route 85 for Putney through Kingston town centre on 8th October 2002. It is followed by one of the very short-lived "split-step" VA class Alexander-bodied Volvo's working route 57 from London United's new Tolworth base.

Some of the last "split-step" double-deckers to operate in London were also members of the last standard London Transport class, the L-class Leyland Olympians. On 28th May 2005, L25 (N) subs for a low-floor VLA as it heads south along Streatham High Road on the resuscitated route 249. This had been reintroduced in May 1991, again replacing the 49's eastern end, this time between Tooting Bec and Crystal Palace. At one time extended as far as Sloane Square at its eastern end, the route now starts at Clapham Common and has been extended beyond Crystal Palace, supplementing the 157 as far as Anerley Station.

Tram Replacement

In common with South East London, South West London kept most of its tram routes until after World War Two, all of which were replaced by motor buses between 1950 and 1952. Now itself long withdrawn, route 181 replaced the original 57A route, which in turn had replaced tram routes 8 and 20 in January 1951 but was effectively renumbered in May 1952. On 25th September 1970, RT1722 (SW) collects passengers in busy Tooting Broadway, on its way from Streatham Garage to Victoria. The route gained O.M.O. SMSs at the beginning of January 1971, later graduating to DMSs. Withdrawn north of Clapham Common in March 1979, the route was discontinued completely in April 1981.

Passing the southern end of Clapham Common itself, RT4323 (AL) heads for Raynes Park on the 189, also a tram replacement, on 21st December 1970. This had replaced tram route 6, and also much of the original bus route 5 which paralleled it between Cannon Street and Clapham Common in January 1951, continuing to Wimbledon and Raynes Park with a rush hour extension to North Cheam. In the November 1958 cuts, it was withdrawn north of Clapham Common but further extended in rush hours to Worcester Park. Not much happened to the route until it converted to DMS O.M.O. six weeks after this picture was taken. Later, it was extended to Hook and Esher, but was then gradually whittled away ending up as a one-bus school route linking Earlsfield and Brixton before being renumbered 689 in 1994.

Also now long defunct, route 95 replaced tram route 10 in January 1951 and it too started at Cannon Street. It ran via Elephant & Castle, Brixton and Streatham to Tooting Broadway. Almost exactly twenty years later, it shared the dubious distinction with route 220 to gain the first of the ill-fated DMSs on 2nd January 1971. This must have been a double whammy for people in the Tooting Broadway area, which both routes served, and on the day before that happened, New Year's Day, 1971, RM865 (BN) loads up with passengers in Tooting Broadway. The 95's conversion to DMS was its death sentence, especially since much of it paralleled the 133 between Streatham and Borough Station, which was still crew operated. It too was gradually whittled away, and finally withdrawn in November 1985, with the 133 being diverted to Tooting to replace it.

Route 109 was one of the best-known tram replacement routes, running all the way from the Embankment loop to Purley down the Brighton Road. It replaced tram routes 16 and 18 in April 1951, running in both directions around the loop via Blackfriars and Westminster Bridges. Introduced with RTs, it briefly had RTWs from Brixton Garage between 1963 and 1966, and on 6th July 1971 more than twenty years after its introduction, RTs rule the roost as RT238 (BN) is one of two running around the block to terminate at Purley. As related with the picture of RM106 on the stand here earlier in the book, the 109 now only runs from Croydon to Brixton, a shadow of its former self!

Replacing the first Kingsway Subway tram route to be withdrawn, the 31, in October 1950, route 170 ran from Wandsworth to Bloomsbury, and then on to Hackney, restoring a link broken when trolleybus route 555 was introduced in 1939. When that too was withdrawn twenty years later, the 170 was extended to replace it, continuing as far as Leyton. It was cut back to Bloomsbury in October 1969, albeit with a rush hour extension to Shoreditch, when "new" bus route 55 was introduced, following the former 555's route and the 55 tram that it had replaced in 1939 between Bloomsbury and Leyton! On 22nd July 1971, RT1708 (WD) passes the working site for the New Covent Garden Market in Nine Elms Lane, four days before this route too converted to DMS. Its northern terminus then was altered to Euston Station, and today the 170 is barely recognisable from its old self, running from Victoria and Roehampton with only a short section in Battersea and Wandsworth "original".

Route 172 replaced tram route 35, one of the last two Kingsway Subway routes in April 1952, originally running from Archway Station to Forest Hill via Islington, Bloomsbury, Westminster Bridge, Elephant and New Cross. For some reason, however, in 1957 it swapped its southern section with the 171 (which had replaced subway tram 33), now running via Kennington, Brixton and Herne Hill to West Norwood. On 4th March 1972, RT809 (Q) heads around the one-way system at St. Matthew's Church, Brixton on its way to Archway. Ruined by being converted from RT to crew DM operation in August 1975, the route enjoyed a brief spell of daily RM operation in 1981/82, before being diverted from Bloomsbury to Kings Cross amid the September 1982 "Law Lords" cuts, and disappearing altogether in 1985.

Route 44 was unique in replacing a tram and trolleybus route at the same time when introduced in October 1950. It replaced the 612 trolleybus between Mitcham and Battersea, Princes Head and then the 12 tram beyond there via Nine Elms, Vauxhall and Albert Embankment to London Bridge. It in fact re-linked the old tram route, the southern end of which the 612 had replaced in 1937! On its last day of crew operation, 16th June 1972, RT2629 (WD) is curtailed at Tooting Southern Region Station when passing through a remarkably deserted Wandsworth town centre. The 44 has also changed drastically since it received O.M.O. DMSs the following day, now running from Tooting to Victoria via Chelsea Bridge and therefore only following its original route between Tooting and Battersea.

Route 168 is another South West London tram replacement route that has long since been withdrawn. Introduced to replace tram route 26 in January 1951, it ran originally from the Embankment to Wandsworth, via Westminster Bridge, Albert Embankment, Vauxhall and Wandsworth Road, with a weekday northward extension to Blackfriars and Farringdon Street. The route gained a southerly extension to Putney Heath in 1958, and then more drastically a northward extension to Turnpike Lane Station in connection with trolleybus replacement in November 1961. The latter was cut back again in January 1965, replaced by a new route 168A, and the 168 itself rerouted via Millbank and Lambeth Bridge. In this view, RT3949 (SW) passes some ghastly 1960s tower blocks in Wandsworth Road on 16th November 1973. RTs gave way to crew DMs at the end of August 1975 and although these were replaced by RMs in December 1980, the 168 was withdrawn just four months later. The 77 (which paralleled it from Clapham Junction to Westminster anyway) was extended in rush hours from Aldwych to Farringdon Street, whilst the 170 replaced its Putney Heath section.

Still recognisable today from its original self since it still runs from Tooting to Elephant & Castle, route 155 replaced tram routes 2 and 4 in January 1951, running from Wimbledon Station to the Embankment via Merton, Tooting, Clapham, Balham, Stockwell and the Elephant, literally above the Northern Line. Latterly withdrawn except in rush hours north of the Elephant and at one time projected all the way to Hersham replacing the 131 and 264 on Sundays, the route converted from RT to RM daily in January 1977, and to O.P.O. in October 1986, two years after receiving crew Ds. Here, RT2737 (AL) crosses Tooting Broadway on its last day of RT operation, 7th January 1977.

Trolleybuses & Their Replacements

Unlike South East London which had just the tail end of route 654 between Croydon and Crystal Palace, and routes 696 and 698 in the Woolwich and Bexleyheath area, a fair number of trolleybus routes penetrated South West London - routes 612, 626, 628, 630 and 655 in the Wandsworth, Clapham Junction and Croydon areas, with of course also the 654, and more importantly, a variety of routes in the Kingston area. The latter were destined to be some of the last to operate, and on their final day, Tuesday 8th May 1962, L3 No. 1446 (FW) heads along Stanley Road, Fulwell bound for Tolworth on route 601. Ironically, this had been London's very first trolleybus route, too.

The Kingston area trolleybus routes were based at Fulwell Depot, from which L3 No.1432 (FW) runs out for a trip on route 667 in the afternoon rush hour of their final day. Trolleybuses had first replaced trams here almost exactly thirty-one years previously.

On 9th May 1962, all but one of Fulwell's trolleybus routes were replaced by new RM-operated services, except for the 604 which ran from Wimbledon to Hampton Court. This was instead replaced by an extension of existing route 131 (which paralleled it between Kingston and Hampton Court anyway) from Kingston to Wimbledon Station, where RT4561 (AL) stands on 11th November 1967. New RMs from Norbiton Garage worked it daily initially, with Merton RTs added at weekends. At various times extending as far out as Hersham Station and as far into Central London as Clapham Common and even Elephant & Castle, the 131 today runs between Kingston and Tooting via Wimbledon.

The two Kingston loop trolleybus routes, 602 and 603, were replaced by bus routes 282 and 283 respectively. The 282 was withdrawn at the end of 1966, but the 283 survived until January 1970. On 21st of that month, three days before its demise, RM732 (NB) calls at Norbiton Station.

On 12th July 1970, RM1768 (FW) has run into Fulwell Garage after working route 267, which ran from Hammersmith to Hampton Court and had replaced trolleybus 667. Numerically, this RM had been burnt out in July 1966, but was "resurrected" using one of two spare RM bodies. The RT on the right is one of those transferred from Twickenham Garage for routes 90 and 90B three months previously when that garage closed.

The most significant penetration trolleybuses made into South West London was that of route 630, which ran all the way from Harlesden to West Croydon through Putney, Wandsworth, Tooting and Mitcham and linked with the otherwise isolated 654 near the end of its journey. It was replaced by bus route 220 in July 1960. That was cut back to Mitcham at the end of 1966 and on 2nd January 1971 suffered being one of the first two routes to receive O.M.O. DMSs. On its final day of RM operation, New Year's Day 1971, RM328 (S) sets down passengers when heading north along Garratt Lane, Tooting.

Illustrating how new links were created when trolleybus routes were replaced, route 285, the 605's replacement, was extended beyond its Teddington terminus to Heathrow Airport. On 23rd March 1971, four days before the route converted to SMS O.M.O., RM1202 (NB) approaches Feltham Station on its way there. The route still links Heathrow and Kingston today.

A once important trolleybus route whose replacement has long since disappeared was the 655, which in its full extent ran from Acton to Hanwell, then down to Brentford and via Chiswick to Hammersmith (thereby in a U-shape), but then continued over Putney Bridge and through Wandsworth to Clapham Junction. It was replaced in November 1960 by bus route 255, which was gradually whittled down over the years until it ran only between Turnham Green and Clapham Junction at the end. On 20th May 1972, RML2651 (R) follows a rag'n'bone man's horse and cart beneath the London & South Western's Windsor and Reading lines in Putney Bridge Road. At this time, Riverside used RMs on it on Mondays to Fridays and RMLs on Saturdays - the route was finally withdrawn four weeks later.

The first trolleybus route serving South West London to be withdrawn under the 1959-1962 Trolleybus Conversion Programme was the 654, running between Crystal Palace and Sutton via Croydon. In stage one of the programme in March 1959, it was replaced by bus route 154, which continued beyond Sutton to Morden Station, alongside the existing 157. The former Sutton Corporation tram depot at Carshalton had been modified for trolleybuses and then adapted for bus operation, but closed in January 1964. On 6th October 1972, RT2669 (A) passes its new offices built upon the introduction of trolleybuses, on its way to Crystal Palace. Route 154 converted to O.M.O. DMS in May 1973, and still links Morden with West Croydon today.

Working route 131's extension over former trolleybus route 604 along West Barnes Lane, Raynes Park, RM1202 (NB) has just passed beneath the London & South Western main line on a short working from Wimbledon to Kingston. RMs have worked this route for just over eleven years, and it is their last day, Friday 11th May 1973. O.M.O. DMSs took over next day.

Route 281 replaced the 601 trolleybus, and was the last of the routes that featured in their final conversion stage to retain RMs. On 14th August 1981, RM1152 (FW) passes a Metrobus on route 267 in King Street, Twickenham on their final day of operation before crew-operated Metrobuses replaced them. The 281 had been extended from its original northern terminus at Twickenham to replace the 73 between there and Hammersmith on Mondays to Saturdays in October 1965. The route still links Hounslow and Tolworth via Kingston today.

Dusk falls on Putney Bridge as DMS1953 (S) loads up on route 220 on its way to Tooting on 28th February 1982. DMSs, which had operated this route since the beginning of January 1971, still struggled on for another eighteen months until replaced by new Metrobuses.

One of route 220's new Metrobuses, M900 (S) has only been in service for twelve days when approaching its Tooting Southern Region Station terminus on 11th September 1983. They would remain on the route until replaced by new low-floor buses in March 2000. Meanwhile, the 220 had been withdrawn south of Wandsworth in May 1991, and still runs between there and Harlesden today.

At Home

One of the most striking bus garages in South West London is that at Stockwell, opened in 1951 for tram replacement services and winning a prize for its design. On 1st April 1967, it was still dominated by RTLs. Parked up are, from left to right, roofbox RTL141, RTL1280, RTL1429 and RTL533. Those working the 2 and 2A were replaced by RMs a few weeks later, and all the others there were ousted by RTs by the end of August. A listed building, Stockwell is still very much in use today.

Sutton Garage is also still in use today, and dates from 1924, originally opened by the London General Omnibus Company. On 1st March 1969, Saunders-bodied RT3927 (A) sets off from it on a trip to Kingston on route 213, which still links the two towns today.

One of London's oldest bus garages, Putney, Chelverton Road is situated to the west of the High Street and was opened originally for horse buses as long ago as 1888, being converted for motor bus operation by the L.G.O.C. in 1912. With its "hole in the wall" entrance in a residential street, it is surprisingly still in use today and on 4th June 1969, itself more than fifty years ago, RML2577 (AF) runs in off route 37. RMLs remained in use here on routes 14 and 22 until July 2005. In contrast, Putney's other garage, on the south side of the bridge, closed in 1958.

Views of the rear of Stockwell Garage are not often illustrated, so here is their RT2390 (SW) there on 15th December 1972, having run in from route 168. Had it not been for the disruption of the tram replacement programme by World War Two, Stockwell (which was a new build and not a former tram depot) would have been a trolleybus depot.

Brixton Garage, opened in 1951, was completely rebuilt on the site of Streatham, Telford Avenue Tram Depot. It was named Brixton to avoid confusion with the existing Streatham Bus Garage further south along the High Road. On the last day of full RT operation on route 133, 22nd March 1975, RT4043 (one of those repurchased from London Country in 1972) sets off on an evening rush hour spreadover duty. RTs however often subbed for the crew DMs which replaced them until removed from the garage in the summer of 1976. Brixton Garage, too, is still in use today.

Long since defunct is the small Kingston Garage in Cromwell Road, which adjoined a covered bus station fronting Clarence Road around the corner. It was opened by the L.G.O.C. in 1922 and remained in use until 2000. It was for many years associated with RFs, which this view of RF389 (K) awaiting departure on a short journey of route 216 to Sunbury Station on 31st May 1975 typifies. In later years, the former coal yard alongside the railway on the other side of Cromwell Road was used for parking buses (and latterly withdrawn ones) and today one of Kingston's two bus stations occupies that site.

Wandsworth Garage started life in 1883 as a tram depot for South London Tramways, later taken over and enlarged by the London County Council. It was partially converted to trolleybus operation in 1937. Thanks to World War Two, the remaining trams there were not replaced until 1950, but by motor buses which replaced the trolleybuses too. On 19th August 1975, RT4119 (WD) is one of two which have been working route 28, presumably subbing for RMs which had replaced them in April 1970. They were based there for route 168, which received crew DMs at the end of the month. The garage closed for normal bus operation in July 1987, but has been retained since early1988 for the Round London Sightseeing Tour fleet.

To supplement the cramped quarters at Kingston Garage, a new garage was opened at nearby Norbiton in 1952, and ten years later, some of the new bus routes that replaced the last trolleybuses were based there. The garage was enlarged in 1984 but, sadly, closed in 1991 thanks to tendering losses brought about by the Thatcher regime's puppet L.R.T. This caused much resentment amongst staff and passengers alike and has neither been forgotten nor forgiven, especially since the splendid modern garage was quickly demolished to make way for a superstore! In happier times, RF440 (NB) stands outside on 25th August 1975.

Streatham Garage, on the High Road just north of Streatham Common, was another L.G.O.C. establishment, opened in 1913. On 29th October 1977, Silver Jubilee SRM9 (AK), alias RM1907, changes crew outside it on route 159, with which the garage was long associated. It was closed for rebuilding in October 1984, reopening in February 1987. However the splendid new garage lasted only until March 1992, again the victim of L.R.T. tendlering policy. Ludicrously used for several years for go-kart racing, with just a tiny corner retained as a terminus for the 159, it was finally demolished a few years ago again to make way for a superstore. What a waste, especially since Brixton Garage just up the road is so overcrowded that the former L.C.C. Brixton Hill tram depot has had to be reopened to take the overflow!

Top: Clapham Garage had an unusual, and ultimately sad, history. Facing the High Road just north of Clapham Common Station, it was completely rebuilt from the tram depot originally opened by London Tramways in 1885 (and later taken over by the L.C.C.) in 1951, but closed only seven years later as a result of the 1958 route cuts. The building was then used by the British Transport Commission between 1960 and 1973 as the Museum of British Transport, incongruously housing not only historic London Transport (and other) public service road vehicles, but also railway locomotives - even including the famous "Mallard". Following the removal of the latter to the new York railway museum, and L.T.'s exhibits to their own museum, the building was used to store new and redundant L.T. buses later in the 1970s, then reopened in 1981 to cover firstly for the rebuilding of Norwood Garage, and then Streatham, but sadly it was not to last, as will be related later. In its first phase of re-use, a smart RM1353 (CA), retaining its Norwood Garage code, is surrounded inside the modern garage by other Routemasters on 28th February 1982. The garage was in an ideal position to operate routes 37 and 137 which passed directly outside it.

Centre: The antiquated Battersea Garage, which occupied both sides of Hester Road just south of Battersea Bridge, dated back to 1906, originally housing vehicles of the London Road Car Company and subsequently passing to the L.G.O.C. The section backing onto the Thames was modernised in 1971 to accommodate DMSs, which operated routes 39 and 39A. On 30th May 1983, new M846 (B) has recently replaced them and stands in Hester Road. The garage was one of the L.R.T. regime's first victims, closing in November 1985. However it reopened in March 1986 to house the Round London Sightseeing fleet, which however moved to Wandsworth in 1988. As related earlier, "yuppie" housing development occupies the site today.

Bottom: At Mortlake Garage, RM1631 (M) sets off on its traditional route 9 for Aldwych on 24th June 1983, the garage's last day of operation. Situated in Avondale Road just to the north of the L.S.W.R. Windsor and Reading lines east of Mortlake Station, it was opened for L.G.O.C. horse buses in 1901, receiving motor buses five years later. Following its closure, at least its southernmost end facing the railway was retained as a bus terminus, the remainder demolished for housing development in what, after all, is a residential street.

The large Merton Garage, dating from 1913 and also opened by the L.G.O.C., is situated alongside the River Wandle on the north side of Merton High Street, and is very much active today, appropriately home to buses of today's London General company. On 1st February 1987, RM713 (AL) runs in dead off route 49 a few months before its conversion to O.P.O.

Clapham Garage in its final guise survived long enough to house the new L-class Leyland Olympians. A couple of days before its final closure, L213 (CA) runs out on 4th February 1987 on route 37, which had converted to O.P.O. the previous June. Is it just coincidence that the "P" has been taken out of the garage name above it? Maybe not, since its strategic site in the centre of Clapham was sold off to house a superstore!